THE COMPLETE SPEECHMAKER

THE COMPLETE
SPEECHMAKER

Peter Eldin, Angela Lansbury
and Jane Willis

WARD LOCK

A WARD LOCK BOOK
First published in the UK 1997 by Ward Lock
Wellington House 125 Strand LONDON WC2R 0BB

A Cassell Imprint

Volume copyright © Ward Lock 1997
Selected text taken from *Speeches and Presentations* copyright © Jane Willis 1996

The Complete Speechmaker has been compiled from *Jokes and Quotes for Speeches* by Peter Eldin, *Wedding Speeches and Toasts* by Angela Lansbury, and *Speeches and Presentations* by Jane Willis, all published by Ward Lock.

Distributed in the United States by Sterling Publishing Co., Inc.
387 Park Avenue South, New York, NY 10016-8810

A British Library Cataloguing-in-Publication Data block for this book may be obtained from the British Library

ISBN 0 7063 7647 1
Printed and bound in Great Britain by Biddles Ltd, Guildford and Kings Lynn

CONTENTS

INTRODUCTION

'You'll have to make a speech!' are words you may wish never to hear. It may be for a wedding, a business lunch or dinner, an informal group, the Parent-teacher Association, a school speech day, or an informal family celebration. But have no fear. Whatever your experience, and despite what you may think, speechmaking can be fun and this book is here to help you.

There are two principal factors involved in the making of a public speaker: there is the person who makes and delivers the speech, and there is the message that the speaker delivers. Some people are naturally more extrovert than others and thrive on audience attention, while others shy away from it and may remember stumbling over a passage they had to read aloud in school. This book will guide you through preparing yourself for standing up in front of both small and large groups of people, and for preparing any material you may need to use if you are giving a business presentation or a talk to a local society.

There are tips and hints on making yourself feel at ease with the situation and on coping with nerves, breathing and voice control exercises, advice on body language, and even suggestions on the type of clothing you should and shouldn't wear. The actual writing of the speech may seem daunting but *The Complete Speechmaker* guides you from your first word to your concluding statement.

One of the problems in giving a speech is finding appropriate jokes and quotes to include. To help with this there are two extensive reference sections which are in subject order and many of the suggestions can be adapted for other situations. If you are searching for material for a wedding speech, for example, do not just refer to the section on weddings and anniversaries. Suitable material will also be found in the section on birthdays. More general jokes and quotes are worth considering for any type of speech, as even areas that have nothing to do with your subject may provide the spark that will lift your speech from predictable run-of-the-mill to something your audience will remember for a long time to come.

Although the general sections of this book will be of use to all, whatever type of speech or presentation being planned, those of you who have been asked to talk at a wedding or celebration will find more advice in Chapter Six. If you are embarking on a business presentation, refer to Chapter Five for specific ideas and suggestions, and guidelines on the use of audio-visual material. Advice for after-dinner speakers can also be found in Chapter Five and those finding themselves with the challenge of chairing a meeting should look for the guidance given in Chapter Four.

'You'll have to make a speech!' – and with the help of this book you'll not only have the confidence to do this but you might even enjoy it as well!

1

PREPARING YOURSELF

The better prepared you are in advance the less agitated and unsure you are likely to feel when the day of giving your speech arrives. Use every opportunity you can to listen and watch any other good speakers. Notice the way they construct and deliver their sentences. The more direct and simple the message, the more readily is it communicated. Listen for eloquence and economy of speech. Shorter sentences hold impact and are easier to grasp than long ones. They also help to discipline the speaker from straying off the point.

Coping with nerves

Whatever the occasion, tell yourself that you are looking forward to making your speech. Keep saying this to yourself until you come to believe it. When you finally stand in front of the audience, say to yourself, 'I'm glad to be here. I wish this to go well for you and for me.' This reinforces feelings of goodwill and will express itself through your body language and voice.

Try the following exercises to help you relax:

Exercise 1 The shoulders

Standing in a relaxed position, lift the shoulders slightly and tense them. Now relax them by letting them fall. Note the difference. Sometimes we lift the shoulders and tense them without realizing that we are doing so. When the shoulders are tensed, the neck becomes tight and we can feel very uncomfortable and tire more easily.

Exercise 2 The neck

Imagine that you have a very long neck. It is perfectly posed between the shoulders which are relaxed and down. Your chin tucks in naturally and with ease. Now move your head gently and with a feeling of elegance turn your head to the left. Next, gently take the head from the left side to the front. Pause. Now gently take the head to the right side and then to the front. Pause.

Imagine being in front of an audience. Repeat the exercise, pretending you are sweeping your listeners with your eyes. Take it slowly and rhythmically, keeping in your mind a feeling of calmness and dignity.

Exercise 3 The head

Imagine that your head is made of granite. In a standing position, let the head slowly, very slowly, fall onto your chest. It feels so heavy that it must succumb to the force of gravity. Keep this feeling with you.

Now for the transformation! Your head is now as light as cotton wool as it floats to an upright position.

Practise this several times to experience the contrast between the feelings of lightness and heaviness.

Exercise 4 A gentle sigh

Standing in a relaxed upright position, inhale slowly and then emit a slow gentle sigh of relief. Think of the sigh as though it were coming from the centre of your body. The shoulders should be down and relaxed. The feeling is one of letting go. As you inhale, place your hands on the lower ribs on either side of your waist and experience the gentle upward and lateral movement of the lower ribs.

Exercise 5 *Concentration*

Choose an interesting or decorative object that appeals to you – an ornament or flower perhaps. Sit in an easy chair with a well-supporting back, and place the object on a table in front of you. Now fix your mind on it. Take in as much detail as you can: colour, texture, shape and so on. Concentrate, giving it your full attention. Now, resting your head against the back of the chair, close your eyes and place the image of that object in your mind. See if you can recall an accurate likeness. When you are ready, open your eyes.

Exercise 6 *Visualizing an entrance*

Use your dining room table and chairs for this one.

Imagine that you are a guest speaker at the meeting. Around the table are seated business associates or wedding guests. They are waiting for you to take your place among them. Carry a folder (if you are imagining a business situation) or gloves (if this is a wedding scenario) and enter the room in a pessimistic manner. Eyes cast down perhaps, the walk uncertain, with rounded or tense shoulders. Walk to the table, place the folder/gloves on it and sit. All your movements suggest lack of confidence and assertiveness.

Repeat the exercise. Again you are very tense and unhappy about the prospect of this meeting or wedding speech. But in this instance it is important that you should on no account lose face. You must be seen to be in charge of the situation. To fail would be unthinkable. Your audience must not see how you feel. You are on the defensive. The body is held stiffly. The shoulders are hunched. The face is set and unsmiling. The walk is stilted. You may cough nervously and play with your tie or necklace as you take a seat at the table. You reach over for a drink of water. Your hands are shaking. Visualize the effect all this might have on the others.

You are now entering the room for the third time. On this occasion you are optimistic and positive. The shoulders are relaxed and down and the head is well balanced between the shoulder blades. The eyes sweep the table where the others are seated and they reflect warmth, interest and enthusiasm. Walking to your seat with purpose and drive you place the folder/gloves on the table. When seated, you rest your arms on the table with hands lightly clasped. You smile pleasantly. It is a smile that has arisen from a knowledge that your feeling of self-esteem is high. It tells the others that you are pleased to be among them and are ready to entertain or do business.

Exercise 7 Recalling a speech

Sit in a chair and think about a speech that you may have heard in the past. In your mind, recall the audience. How did they react to the talk? Did they appear happy and satisfied or bored and restless? Was the speaker attractive in appearance and manner? If so, why? How did he or she move? Was the voice interesting? Was a message communicated that was clear and concise? Were there amusing breaks, offering light relief?

Now imagine that it is you giving the speech in place of the speaker. It may be a similar talk, given to the same audience. How would you like to be seen? Try to see yourself through the eyes of that audience. Listen to their needs. Think it through stage by stage from the entrance, when you walk to the platform, or rise from your seat, to applause at the end.

Breath and the voice

Breathing for any form of speech is a natural function that we don't normally think about. However, paying it some attention is necessary for those who find it difficult to project their voices easily when speaking in public.

To be heard while addressing an audience, we need to create space in the throat and chest so that the required amount of air is directed through the vibrating vocal chords. The throat, mouth and nose help us to amplify our sound, which would be less audible if it did not pass through these resonators. The mouth and throat should therefore be free of tension, and the nose kept clear and unblocked, in order for the resonators to function effectively. These exercises will help your breath control:

Exercise 8 Breathing in

Stand straight but not stiffly. This is important, as good alignment will help promote strong voice production. Remember when you inhale not to raise your shoulders. Doing so will encourage tension in the neck, throat and breathing muscles.

Now feel your ribcage. Ribs form the thorax and are attached at the back to the twelve thoracic vertebrae. Rest one hand on your midriff and the other on your lower ribs that reach round the waist. Breathe in slowly and notice how the hand resting on the midriff moves out slightly. This has happened because the diaphragm, which is a muscular partition that separates the thorax from the abdomen, has contracted and flattened, thereby pushing the belly outwards. Because the lower ribs are more flexible than those higher up, they will flex upwards and outwards by the use of the intercostal muscles that are attached to them.

This muscular activity expands the chest cavity, creating more space for the lungs to fill with air, which is drawn into them through the windpipe, nose and/or mouth.

Exercise 9 Breathing out

Now breathe out slowly and feel the lower ribs gradually relax as the lungs contract, the diaphragm rises and the midriff or belly moves inwards. As this is happening, the transverse abdominal muscles are gently drawn inwards. This contraction of the abdominal muscles is used to help our outgoing breath when we speak, gently supporting the diaphragm and lower ribs, so that sound can be sustained and energized.

Remember: breath in, hand on midriff moves outwards; breath out, hand moves inwards.

Because it is on the outgoing breath that we speak, we aim to balance breath with sound. The moment we start to exhale, we need to use the voice. Aim to achieve this smoothness in the following exercise (Exercise 10). Practising regularly and for short periods should help give you the breath control that is needed when speaking in front of an audience.

Physical tensions and feelings of nervousness may be increased, or even caused by the insufficient intake of air; at times this can result in a sore throat, breathy or strained voice and tailing off at the ends of sentences. Some speakers do not allow themselves breathing space! They take in small gasps of air and do not take advantage of their breathing muscles. The shoulders may rise on inhalation, which encourages the ribs to move in one way only – vertically – and this can constrict the breath. The ribs need to flex vertically and laterally. Raising the arms slightly to the side while practising breathing in may provide a picture of opening out, so that lateral expansion is encouraged.

Exercise 10 Humming

HUM. This is a very resonant sound. As you do this become aware of the vibrations by touching your throat, lips and nose. Now, taking a full breath, increase the volume of the hum. Finally, begin softly and gradually increase the volume until quite loud. Stay relaxed, avoid strain and rest in between exercises.

Exercise 11 Hoorah!

Take the word HOORAH! Repeat it several times with freedom and spontaneity. This is a valuable exercise as an aid for overcoming inhibitions. Use your arm to guide your sound forward and have fun with it!

Exercise 12 Sound from your centre

Imagine the sound rising naturally from your midriff or centre as you speak the following sentences. Allow your thoughts to guide the sense of what you are saying. Remember to pause and breathe after each sentence.

1 I am relaxed and confident.

2 My neck is free of tension.

3 I am filling my body with energy.

4 I am releasing my sound into the room.

5 I shall be heard.

The power behind your voice

When speaking in public, the voice needs to be strong without strain or shouting. Your breath is the power behind your voice. Imagine a string of pearls. The string has to be long enough to support the pearls but if that string is weak and breaks, the pearls will scatter all over the floor. So it is with the voice. The string is the breath and the pearls are the words. There must therefore be enough breath-power behind the voice to support the words, otherwise the air will run out and the voice falter and fade. It is important to inhale as much air as necessary. The aim is to flow and we breathe where there are natural pauses in the text.

In order to make sense of content, learn where to punctuate your speech and phrase your words. Do not break your phrases or your speech will become jerky and the sense may be lost.

When your speech is prepared, rehearse it aloud, and initially gauge where you are going to take:

a) your full-stop pauses (remember you will pause longer and take a fuller breath at your full-stop break) and

b) your comma pauses and supplementary breaths.

Speak the following exercise. Use this sign / for a comma breath pause and // for a full-stop breath pause.

As you take your breaths during this exercise, imagine that they are gently dropping into the centre of your body, at the waist. Breathe out with the words, aiming to keep the voice sustained all the while. To help you, rest a hand on your midriff as you do this.

Ensure that you are standing straight but be at ease, especially around the top part of your body, the neck, throat and shoulders, which should be relaxed and down. Stand with legs slightly apart, the weight evenly distributed on both feet. Your head needs to be well balanced between the shoulder blades. The chin should not jut out or be pushed too far into the neck. If you were speaking to a fairly large audience you would need to speak a little slower and very clearly.

Exercise 13 *Phrasing and pausing 1: Jersey*

The state of Jersey is a part of the Channel Islands / and is twelve miles from the coast of France. //

Physical features resemble a mixture of Normandy in France, / and the county of Wiltshire in England. //

The island is small: / nine miles by five, / and divided into twelve parishes. //

Villages are picturesque, / comprising stone-built farms and well-kept houses. //

Winding roads are flanked on either side by soft rolling country-side, / small sheltered bays and natural harbours. //

The chief industry is market gardening; / and it is on this island that the well-known Jersey cow is reared. //

French influence on Jersey is reflected in the names of the roads, / and of some farms and houses. //

Although Jersey is a self-run state, / having its own legislative assemblies and legal systems, / it still remains part of the British Isles. //

In 1941 Jersey was invaded and occupied by the German forces, / who remained there until 1945 and the ending of the war. //

Exercise 14 Phrasing and pausing 2: The secretary bird

The secretary bird is an African bird of prey. //

It gets its name from the crest of long feathers on top of its head which resemble the old quill pens. //

The plumage is grey and white, / with black hindquarters and black and white bars on the tail. //

It stands four feet tall, / has very long legs and a two-foot long tail. //

Secretary birds feed mainly on insects, / lizards and small snakes. //

The nest is built of sticks and clay, / and is used over a period of a few years. //

The large eggs are laid in August. //

When they are hatched, / the young birds do not leave the nest for about five months. //

Although secretary birds are powerful fliers, / they spend a great deal of their time on the ground. //

Before practising the next exercise, mark where you are going to place your breath pauses. Some of the sentences are quite long and require good breath support.

Exercise 15 Phrasing and pausing 3: The jay

The history and grandeur of England have rested on one bird, the jay. If it were not for this beautiful creature, Henry VIII's great navy could not have set sail to conquer and help build the great British Empire. For it is the jay that is responsible for the propagation of the English oak, being the only species that commonly plants acorns. This is because, unlike the squirrel, it does not bite off the fruit's tip, thus preventing germination.

There are more exercises to help you in developing ability to phrase and pause in Chapter Three.

Using the muscles of the face

Exercises 16 and 17 will help to develop strong and flexible facial muscles.

Use a mirror to ensure that you are working the lip muscles. With the sound **W** as in **will**, the lips need to be brought well forward into a small circle. For the **ee** sound as in the word **we**, the lips need to be gently drawn back as though you are giving someone a soft smile. Avoid overstretching the mouth as this will create tension, the very thing you need to avoid. Thorough but gentle exercise is what is needed. The same principles apply to the piece of verse. These exercises should be practised regularly prior to a public-speaking engagement.

Exercise 16 Mouth and lip muscles

1 Make a wide grin and then bring the lips well forward into a pout.

2 Blow out through the lips like a baby.

3 Repeat the following:
Will we, will we, will we, wind down the window for
  Wilfred?
Wendy and Winifred, Wendy and Winifred.
Willy and Wendy and Winifred.

4 Mime the following poem by over-emphasizing the lip movements to gain full mobility of the mouth. This is important. Repeat using the voice. Speak it with expression and animation.

WEATHER TALK

'Isn't it cold? Look at that rain!'
Stating the obvious time and again.
What should I answer?
'Yes, I can see!'
Really much easier to simply agree.

'Nicer today.' Nicer than what?
Oh, talk of the weather! (I almost forgot.)
'Yes, nicer indeed,'
I quickly assent
And almost as quickly I start to relent.

For what are you thinking?
Are you thinking as I –
'Don't talk of the weather,
Don't dwell on the sky.
Conventional, proper –
So socially right.
Much nicer to speak of the things that delight.'

Remember to use your mouth – you'll be clearer and understood.
It is the consonants that provide the outline and cut to your words.
No matter how well a person projects their voice, if the word endings are weak, they won't be heard or understood. So remember:
clarity aids projection. In particular, watch for:

　　t, d, m, n, l and k endings: e.g. tent, David, kick
　　t, k, l, in the middle of words: e.g. butter, licking, illness.

Lazy tongues make lazy speech

While consonants give clarity and cut to a word, vowels give tonal
quality to the voice. Because this book is not an elocution manual,
the formation of vowels and consonants will not be dealt with in
intricate detail. Suffice to say that a consonant is formed by air

19

coming from the larynx that is stopped by one or two of the articulative organs of speech – tongue, teeth, hard and soft palates, gums, lips – before it is released. For example, **d** requires that the vocalized breath from the larynx is stopped by the tongue-tip against the teeth ridge (the ridge formed behind the upper teeth), before being released as the sound **d**. **b** requires that the vocalized breath is stopped by the lips, before being released as the sound **b**. Other vocalized consonants are: **m, g, l, ge, n, ng, r, th, v, w, y** and **z**. Some consonants use vocalized breath and some unvocalized, such as **k**. This requires unvocalized breath from the larynx being stopped by the back of the tongue arching towards the soft palate and then releasing. **p** is another unvocalized consonant, as are: **ch, f, h, sh, s, t,** and **th**. These need particular care while enunciating. You will see that **th** appears in both lists, unvocalized as in: **Thursday, thanks, theatre,** or vocalized as in: **this, that, there, those, than**.

Vowels on the other hand have a free, open passage. The lips and tongue shape the different sounds, but there is no truncation.

Make your consonants distinctly, and for the formation of the vowels, open your mouth to let out the sounds. Keep the jaw flexible. There should be a concept of placing vowel sounds forward in the mouth. Shaping the lips will help you achieve this.

The following exercises incorporate the vowels and some of the consonants. Aim for accuracy and expressive delivery. Using generous mouth movements will exercise the muscles and help loosen the jaw. However, avoid strain, as this can be counter-productive. These exercises should be practised regularly prior to a public-speaking engagement.

Exercise 17 Lip and tongue warm-ups

Speak the following clearly and with energy. Aim for accuracy. When familiar with them, repeat with speed until you can speak them quickly without making a mistake.

Use firm tongue and lip movements to exercise the muscles, but avoid strain.

d d d t t t (Repeat 3 times)

l l l k k k (Repeat 3 times)

m m m n n n (Repeat 3 times)

b b b p p p (Repeat 3 times)

tot dod lel nell

tok tuk tak tek

lot lad led men

bold helm land doubled

better botter batter bitter

heckle locker lacquer liquor

meddled modelled middled troubled

bep bap bip bop

kep kap kip kop

Stack the sacks and check the stock

'Double, double, toil and trouble'

Peter Piper picked a peck of pickled pepper

The old kitchen clock has stopped

Exercise 18 Articulation for short vowels plus consonants

a   Angela is angry with Andy for antagonizing her Alsatian.

b   Betty and Bill are Benny's best friends.

c   Cats catch and kill canaries.

d   Dennis and Dave drive dangerously down Dudden Hill.

e   Eddie is extrovert, extravagant and entertaining.

f   Flat fish and flying fish; fillet of fish and fish cakes.

g   Ghastly Gordon greedily gobbles gherkins.

h   Henry has a hundred hats hanging on his hat stand.

i   Ingrid invites in-laws to Ipswich.

j   Jolly Jasper jumps for joy.

k   Kit eats Kit-Kat in Kerry's kitchen.

l   Lady Lavinia Luckham listens to Liszt.

m   Mermaids' melodies are mesmerizing.

n   Nattie's neighbours niggle noisily.

o   Opulent Olive enjoys opera and oratorios.

p   Pots, pans, powder and prunes.

qu   Quirky quacks quibble and quip.

r   Running Richard races rogues round Rotten Row.

s   Sally's sister Susie sambas.

t   Trains, tickets and timetables are terribly trying.

u   Uncle Ulric unfolds his umber umbrella.

u   Puss chased the rooks by the brook in the wood.

v   Vain Vinny varnishes vases with vivid violet.

w   Wandering wenches wear wellingtons in wintry weather.

x   Xavier's X-rays are excellent.

y   Yokels yodel at Yuletide.

z   Zig-zagging, zany zebras.

Exercise 19 Articulation for long vowels

ah   Arnold, Jaguar, far, smarter, car, Carl, Ferrari
Arnold's Jaguar is a far smarter car than Carl's Ferrari.

er   early, bird, worm
The early bird catches the worm.

aw   wardrobes, warm, ward, hoary, storm
Wardrobes must be warm, to ward off hoary frost and storm.

oo   goosey, soup, rooster, cook, mousse, noodle
Goosey soup, rooster soup, cool mousse and noodle soup.

ee   sleepy, dreamy, easy, stream
Sleepy, dreamy, take it easy; swim with the stream.

ew   new, tulips, Duke, Tewkesbury
The new tulips were given to the Duke when he visited
Tewkesbury.

ay   pale, maidens, bathe, daily, shady, glades
Pale maidens bathe daily in the shady glades.

i   nice, rice, light, white
Nice rice, light rice, nice, white, light rice.

oy   toys, boys
Men with toys will always be boys.

ow   Brown, found, cow, lounge
Mrs Brown found a cow in her front lounge.

oh   Roland, wrote, odious, odes, Rhoda
Roland wrote odious odes to Rhoda.

ear   piercing, cheers, weary, ears
Piercing cheers make weary ears.

air   aeroplanes, heiresses, various, fair
Aeroplanes fly heiresses to various fair places.

23

oor   rural, tours, brochure
Rural Tours are advertising their brochures.

ure   Muriel, liqueur, ewer
Muriel hides bottles of liqueur in the bathroom ewer.

ire   choirs, lyres, friars
Harmonizing choirs; lutes and lyres; monks and friars.

our   flowers, showery, bowers
Seeds burst into flowers in showery bowers.

Limber up your language skills

'Language is the dress of thought.'
   (Samuel Johnson, *Life of Cowley*)

Exercise 20 Speaking with clarity

For the person who is a newcomer to public speaking, the task of channelling thoughts and setting them down on paper in an expressive fashion can be extremely difficult. The brain needs a prompt, some kind of stimulus to get it going in the direction for which it is intended. There needs to be a limbering-up period. Just as with keeping fit, the warming-up before exercise and the warming-down afterwards is considered essential in order to prevent undue stress on the body. And so exercises that encourage language skills can help fluency of speech.

The following exercises will encourage oral skills. They are meant to be fun and, like games, you can play them singly, with a partner, or with members of your family. The exercises encourage imagination, accuracy and concentration. They all require self-involvement.

When practising these exercises, avoid over-use of the same word. For example, lovely. Alternatives might be: pleasing, elegant, graceful, fair, brilliant, radiant, etc. Choose expressive vocabulary that adds colour and enhances your descriptions. A thesaurus provides a wealth of alternative adjectives that you can use. (There is more advice in Chapter Two on choosing words well.)

Exercise 21 Visualization

This exercise or game can be practised alone, with a partner or within a group.

Sit back in a comfortable chair and close your eyes. Take your mind back to a place you have visited. Maybe it was while on holiday at the seaside, or in the mountains; a cathedral, house or park. Take time to recall the place as accurately as you can. When you are ready, recount this memory aloud, either to yourself or to your partner. Having described the place, express your feelings about it. Why did you choose it? What was it that held special appeal for you? If at first you find this exercise difficult, start by describing some functional tasks, such as cooking breakfast, your journey to work, cleaning the car, etc. Focusing on detail can improve concentration skills – vital for public speaking.

If you are doing this exercise with a partner or group, take turns, and while one is recounting their scene, use your listening and concentration to help draw on your imagination to create as full a picture in your mind as possible of the speaker's account.

This exercise can be developed into story-telling. Choose a scene, such as a walk through the woods, or a visit to an art gallery. As before, sit with eyes closed and imagine yourself as a character within this scene. It can then be developed by each member of the group in turn. Avoid too much plot-mongering and centre your attention on the characters and the situations that evolve from them.

When the story is completed, write it down and read it aloud. Your thoughts and creative ideas have now become manifest. You have used your imaginative skills to formulate a story which has been processed from a memory or an idea. This has been expressed verbally, and then translated into the written word.

A similar development takes place when preparing and delivering a speech. You are given a theme or subject on which to talk. Your imagination then sets to work on ways to present your ideas creatively. Collation of the relevant material comes next, which is then transposed onto paper, and finally delivered as a speech.

Exercise 22 Story-telling from pictures

Nowadays there are so many beautiful greeting cards on the market. Begin by collecting a few of these to use for this exercise. Choose those that appeal to you and are interesting in content, such as reproductions of paintings, preferably with people in them.

Choose a quiet moment, relax in a chair, place one of these cards in front of you and study it. Look at the colour and texture, the shapes and contents of the card. Now describe what you see.

When you have studied the card, become more involved with the subject matter. Imagine stepping into the picture. For example, the card might depict a family sitting or playing on the beach. Envisage yourself as a member of that family, a guest, or passer-by. Establish what your relationship is within that group, and observe what might be going on around you. Speak your thoughts.

As you become more confident with this exercise, you can use a tape-recorder to monitor your use of language and vocabulary. Play the tape back and assess yourself for fluency and accuracy.

Speech-makers are very often remembered for the stories they tell. For them, they are a welcome tool, and part of an essential kit. A well-rendered anecdote can bear the stamp of its speaker.

A development of this exercise, which you can play alone or with a partner, uses several cards.

A arranges a selection of cards in any order he or she chooses. B weaves a story following the sequence in which the cards are placed.

Exercise 23 Reading and retelling a story

This exercise encourages memory, accuracy and concentration skills.

Read aloud a short fairy story or the like.

Retell it, using your own words.

Exercise 24 Reading on tape

You may prefer to read your text aloud when giving a speech. If this is so, check your ability to sight-read by taping yourself speaking a passage of text. If on playback you think it lacks flow and is verbally inaccurate, then your sight-reading is weak and would benefit from practice.

For business presentations, precision can be essential. Read aloud a little every day and your confidence and skill will increase.

Note the following:

1 Mark where you are going to take your breath pauses. This will help your flow.

2 Aim to glance ahead when you are reading, so that your peripheral vision is aware of the text before you speak it.

3 When checking your recorded passage against your written text, methodically underline words that have been mispronounced or left out, and then repeat the same exercise until you get it right.

4 When preparing your presentation, ensure that you underline words that you find difficult to pronounce. Rehearse these repeatedly until you feel comfortable saying them.

2

PREPARING AND PLANNING

'Tongues in trees, books in running brooks, sermons in stones, and good in everything.' (Shakespeare, *As You Like It*, Act II, i)

'I feel,' said Mr Toot, in an impassioned tone, 'as if I could express my feelings, at the present moment, in a most remarkable manner, if – if – I could only get a start.' (Charles Dickens, *Dombey and Son*, Chapter 56)

When first sitting down to write your speech, it may be a good idea to ask yourself why you've been asked to speak. Are you the father of the bride? Perhaps you are an expert on local history? Is it because you are an extrovert and known for being humorous? Or is this a business presentation to be made to gain new business or inform your staff? Whatever your purpose, the only way to give your best is by being prepared.

Planning your speech

One of the most important rules, and one ignored by a great many people, is to prepare well in advance.

Even if you are an expert on a subject you will not give of your best if you try to talk off the cuff. As soon as you know you are going to give a speech, start to work on it. Give yourself enough time to consider what you want to say, to do any research necessary, write your speech, gather together any visual aids (see Chapter Five for guidance about using these), rehearse it and to perform any last minute pruning. Remember, a few scribbled notes will not suffice.

Length

It is important to decide the length of your speech before beginning to research and write it. Too short and it may seem rude, too long and it may bore your audience (and perhaps even dampen the proceedings at a celebration). If you are working on a business presentation, the exact subject area may dictate how long you will be talking for. But for many occasions, including less formal business ones, the traditional advice of 'leave 'em asking for more' applies. In other words do not go on for too long and outstay your welcome. 'Stand up, speak up, then shut up' is the best advice that all speakers would do well to remember.

Consider your audience

Bear in mind the type of audience you will have and slant your material towards them. The same is also true of the occasion – no one wants a humorous speech at a funeral! You must judge your audience and construct your speech accordingly.

Obtaining material

If you are to make a speech on a particular subject your own knowledge of that subject will provide your first source of infor- mation. Get a large sheet of paper and note down everything you can think of that will be relevant to your speech. As you go about your daily work, write down on paper any ideas that spring to mind and file them away. Apart from saving yourself work later on, having some initial material provides a comforting buffer when you come to start writing.

Thinking before writing

Before you start to write, here are some specific points to consider:

1 Know what your subject is to be and how far you are going to take it. (More specific guidance for business presentations, weddings and other celebrations, and after-dinner speaking, is given in the relevant chapters.)

2 Ask yourself, 'What do the audience really want to know?'

3 Will the important facts be highlighted?

4 Will the talk be clear and easy to understand?

5 Is there a strong theme throughout? (Avoid too much padding or deviating from the point.)

6 Will there be a time limit (see above)? Check that you will be able to keep to it.

7 Will it be possible to introduce pictorial language? Is it too abstract?

8 Will the speech be presented in such a way that listeners will find it easy to retain?

9 Is there too much information?

10 Will you use visual aids? Where will they fit in? Will the venue be set up for them? (See Chapter Five for advice on using visual aids.)

Remember to:

11 Use simple and direct language wherever possible.

12 Be grammatical and clear in delivery.

13 Adopt a bright and cheerful style, without being trite or trivial.

It's important to speak the language your audience will understand. If you are to make a speech to an audience who know relatively little about your subject, using highly technical jargon will fog the listeners and lose their interest. But pepper your talk with personal experiences and stories and you will highlight your message and illustrate the technical points in a simple and uncomplicated way. On the other hand, you may be talking to a professional group of colleagues, in which case more detailed technicalities will not be out of place although you should be warned off overloading the listeners with too much data. The brain can only absorb so much at any one time.

Talking in pictures will improve the ambience. Look for places where you can lighten with pictorial colour. If you dislike telling a joke for fear of it falling flat (see Chapter Seven for more advice about this), tell a story instead. It will add charm and zest to your speech.

Developing your powers of imagery

Read the phrases below and open your mind to the various images they suggest. Picture them as you read aloud the following:

Bright buttoned stars.
Melting moments.
Vibrating motorways.
Steep steps.
Wold-wooded Worcestershire.
Fast and slick.
Momentous moment.
Monotonous monologue.
Energetic exercises.
Marked improvement.
Chocolate truffles.
Thrilling races.
Massive machinery.
Reverent rituals.

Happy holiday.
Mouth-watering dessert.
Slide and kick.
Soft chiffon.
Flat feet.
Jet fighter.
Snappy dresser.
Wellington weather.
Violent storms.
Parking ticket.
Ground to a halt.
Ready, steady, go!
Terribly tired.
The beginning, the end.

Figures of speech that can be used for impact

Metaphors and similes

These can stimulate audience imagination, and add speech impact. Use them sparingly and with discretion for maximum impact.

Avoid mixing metaphors, such as in the following. 'Gentlemen, the seed of disharmony has been sown among us. If it is not nipped in the bud, it will burst into a huge blaze that will flood the whole planet.'

Rhetorical questions

The speaker appeals directly to the audience by asking a question that does not demand a reply. This can be used to intensify dramatic impact and involves the speaker more closely with the audience. For example:

'Why are we here today? We are here to address the problem of litter in our community.'

'What are the main principles of a marriage?'

If you are planning to use this form of emphasis, ensure that the inflection of your voice does not rise on the question, but rather ends on a downward note. The former method demands an answer, whereas the latter does not.

Antithesis

By focusing on contrasts, this is used to set one idea against another. For example:

'You played with him; I worked with him.'

'You taught; I was your student.'

'You go; we stay.'

Repetition

By using this, points of issue can be reinforced. For example:

'We will win. We will win, not lose.'

'Pause awhile and think; think what this will mean.'

Words and phrases to avoid

With the exception of certain wedding receptions, avoid using affected terms such as:

'on this *auspicious* occasion'

'this most *prestigious* building'

'my *grateful* thanks'

'*would like to say a few words*' (When you mean '*make a speech*' or '*give a talk on*'.)

'*very pleased*' (*Pleased* is sufficient.)

'*those ones*' (*Those* and *ones* mean the same.)

'*sole monopoly*' (*Sole* and *monopoly* mean the same.)

'*actually*', '*frankly*', '*as a matter of fact*' (Superfluous words.)

Clichés and superfluous expressions

Try to avoid these. Some examples are:

sort of; kinda; you know; I mean; in this day and age; basically speaking; tell me about it; by and large; be that as it may; the fact of the matter is; at the end of the day; let's face it; all things considered; to be honest; fair enough; same difference; just one of those things.

The other danger with clichés, particularly at weddings and celebrations, when you might be tempted to say 'May all their troubles be little ones' is that older members of the audience may have heard them before and indeed the previous speaker may use the same joke or saying.

The plan of your speech

The following guidelines are to help you plan a speech for a social occasion, such as a meeting of a club or society, when your approach to your audience needs to be friendly and informal. However, the formats for social and business presentations are generally similar, with a few possible variations:

1 A business presentation may need to contain more compacted information, with the additional back-up of visual aids and handouts.

2 There can be a greater need for precision and more sharply focused material, with occasional summaries to ensure clarity.

3 There may be more statements of facts – e.g. statistics and data information.

4 Introductions may be minimal in content, stating briefly but clearly and with vitality the areas that are to be covered and how they will be broached. This may apply more readily to presentations given within a company and among colleagues.

(For guidance on business presentations, please refer to Chapter Five.)

Like most human endeavours, a speech needs a beginning, a middle and an ending. In the introduction, you are establishing contact with the audience and indicating the theme of your talk; in the middle, you are giving the main information; in the conclusion you are drawing the threads together and reiterating the most important points. In other words, as someone once said, 'First I tell 'em what I'm going to tell 'em. Then I tell 'em. Then I tell 'em what I've told them.'

Introduction

Think of your introduction in two parts.

Part A: 'Getting to know you' time

Imagine that there is an invisible thread connecting you with the listeners. So: start on familiar ground, with something that they know. For example, you can connect through a story, a current event, or a television programme. It will encourage them to think, 'Oh yes, I remember that', or 'Oh yes, I've been there'.

Introductions should be attractive. They don't need to be startlingly dramatic, but they should aim at being imaginative. That way the audience will want more. Talk to the listeners in a conversational and warm manner. Imagine that you are speaking to a close friend who is sitting at the back of the hall. This is an example of a Part A introduction on the advantages of a microwave oven:

'I've had a hectic day at the office. Everything that could have gone wrong – has! The important client I've been expecting all week failed to turn up. My colleague is in a foul mood and the office lease has finally run out.

I arrive home wet through and exhausted, after waiting one hour for the number 72 bus, which appears to be the last bus in the world! I make for the kitchen and a much-anticipated gin and tonic, only to find that the tonic is not only warm but flat. My family keep mentioning a word called 'Food'. All I want to do is sleep! But I stoically stir myself and make for the freezer. Thank heavens for fish fingers!

'What, fish fingers again?' their eyes plead. 'Then we'll have steak,' I say cheerily, and I plonk a large misshapen block of frozen meat onto the draining board. Thank heavens for the microwave!

The freezer has not transformed my way of life. Rather it has increased my feelings of inadequacy. The thought of a 'Supermarket in my own home' does not charge me with enthusiasm. But the microwave oven is my friend and ally!'

Part B: Tee-off time!

You are now in a position to lead them onto new ground. From the familiar, you can now gently lead them to the unfamiliar.

'By using the Auto Defrost, you can thaw meat, fish or poultry by their weight. Whereas before I bought my microwave oven, it took hours to defrost food, now it takes only minutes. The steak is in the frying pan in no time. What a time saver!

Microwaves have other advantages too ...'

The body of the speech

The main facts and/or arguments go into this section.

Some people find it easier to write the body of the speech first, followed by the conclusion. They then insert the introduction last of all. For the first draft this may be the easier way. It is a matter of choice.

Know how long the speech will run. If time is short, the talk should be balanced in such a way that the audience is not overloaded with too many details. A longer speech, however, may handle more information.

Make the most forceful point of argument last. This gives weight to the speech. It will also assist delivery when building the talk to a climax.

If a speech is well structured in content (like a well-written poem), it will trace itself through the various nuances, guiding the speaker to perform at his or her best.

Building to a climax

The climax is the site of greatest interest, achieved via the arrangement of points addressed in ascending order, and culminating in an acme of ideas.

When you come to deliver the speech, the thoughts should precede the words. It is the increased intensity of thought, allied with necessary modulations of pitch, pause, power, emphasis and pace, that lead to the climax.

Exercise 25 Building to a climax

Practise the following. Use thought to guide your voice, emphasis to underline meaning, and increased pace, power and intensity in accordance with the action.

1 John climbed the chestnut tree.
  Higher and higher he went
  Until he reached the very top.

2 Alec stuck the firework into the earth. The paper smouldered, the powder ignited, there was a rapid build-up of pressure in the rocket case, and the hot gases were expelled rearwards. With a sudden burst of light, the rocket was launched – WHOOSH!

3 If we are to succeed,
  If we are to win the race against time,
  We must act now,
  And we must act fast!

The conclusion

Audiences need to be reminded. Recapitulation is especially valuable for business speeches. However, if the talk is very inspirational or anecdotal, too much reminding may weaken its effect. In that case you may like to give a brief conclusion.

Towards the end of the talk, slow down the delivery to allow the audience time to realize that you are drawing to a close. Never fade out by weakening the voice. Keep it strong and sure.

Leave the listeners with something to remember, not just by the content of your speech but by your delivery and attitude.

The first draft

Now you are ready to start writing your speech. You need to have a genuine interest in the topic on which you are to speak. Make it your own from the beginning. This can help stimulate the brain and get it moving. Your thoughts, your ideas help to create a personal touch which can in turn generate enthusiasm, a looking forward and a wish to do well. If a talk is based purely on the accumulation of knowledge acquired solely from books, your speech may lack lustre and personal magnetism. Begin by jotting down your own ideas and build from there.

Choose a time of day when you can work without interruption. Sit down and start writing, using any collated material that appeals and which you think is relevant. If a fact or an idea reminds you of a story, write it down. At this early stage you can allow your mind the freedom of expression. Whether or not you use all the material written at this time is not so important. The important factor is to get started and to create. The imagination may be inhibited if too many boundaries are introduced too early.

Develop the habit of writing in the way in which you speak, because it is you that your audience wants to hear. It may also help your ideas to flow more easily.

The second draft

This is the stage at which you groom your speech. Before you begin, reread your first draft and then ask yourself:

1 How do I view myself?

2 Who are my audience?

3 How do I view them?

4 How would I like them to view me?

5 What will my audience gain from my speech?

6 What do I hope to gain from my speech?

These points are ways of helping you to link with your audience before you've even seen them. Keep these thoughts at the back of your mind as you prepare your second draft.

Now you are in the strong position of directing your speech in the way in which you would like it to go. The groundwork has been prepared in draft one and you are ready to move on.

You may at this stage of development need to rewrite most of your existing material. However, with the main ideas of your speech set down on paper in the first draft, this should not prove to be such a daunting task, and with writing practice these skills can improve. Now is the time to determine an outline. You might ask yourself, 'What is my theme? How far do I want to take it?' Keep within the parameters that you set yourself. In the original draft you tapped your creative skills by permitting yourself to think on all sides of your subject. Now you can afford to discipline your work and thus build a format, without being in danger of losing the heart of your speech and the spontaneity of your ideas.

Rather like a play or a novel, a speech needs a beginning, a middle and an end. Because you have written the first draft, most of your material and the substance of your speech are probably all there, and just need to be moulded into an attractive shape. If you decide to work on the middle of your talk first, remember that ideas or arguments need to be arranged so that one flows into another in an organized, smooth way. They can also be set out in order of importance. A well-structured speech is rather like a chain, whereby one link is fastened to the next. A speech written with this in mind will possess flow and also help put the audience at their ease. They will relax and so be able to concentrate more easily on what is being said.

Keep your message clear and simple without appearing patronizing or condescending in your approach. Be direct, positive and to the point without any abruptness. The syntax can influence the way in which a speech is delivered, so write it in a warm manner, one that can be translated into cheerful speech. Add a little colour by telling a story. This can also help to re-engage flagging interest. It is a good standby prop, an important ingredient to add at a strategic place in a speech that may possess rather dry material. (This can be a useful addition for business presentations. Please refer to Chapter Five for more information.)

Avoid overloading a speech with too much information as this can be difficult for an audience to retain. If there is a necessity to provide copious facts, figures, statistics, etc. you can give handouts where and when appropriate, or as an addition to visual aids. Make a note of where you are going to use your visual aids and/or handout sheets and demonstration objects.

When the second draft is completed, put it away in a drawer and forget it for a few days. Come back to it at a later date and you will review it afresh. This is the time to edit your speech and delete unnecessary material. Remember that a short, well-structured speech is preferable to one that is longer but less memorable.

Tape-record your speech, listen to yourself objectively and criticize your format from that. This also provides a good opportunity to time it and any alterations in length or pace of delivery can now be made.

Starting and finishing – a reminder

The introduction to your speech is dealt with on pages 35–6. But it is worth mentioning that you may find it easier to write it last of all. An introduction may spring more easily to mind once you have completed your written work. Reading through your material will provide mental pictures to help and guide you towards writing an opening. Remember, your opening remarks set both the tone of your speech and the reaction you will get from your audience. The closing remarks round off the speech and bring your talk to a definite end. It's a bad idea to try to memorise your entire speech (and perhaps an impossibility) but the opening and closing remarks are an exception to this rule. If you memorize your opening comments you start without hesitation and this will give you confidence in your performance. Similarly, a memorized closing remark rounds off the speech and might even provide the cue for applause!

The final draft

By the time you reach this third and final stage of written preparation, you will be quite familiar with the text of your speech. You may feel that on the day of the presentation you will be prepared and ready to read it out aloud. On some occasions, such as business presentations (see Chapter Five) this may be appropriate or even necessary and there are suggestions for doing this on page 27. However, there is another way. Many speakers transcribe the main topics of the material onto postcards. These are known as prompt cards. They enable you to refer to major points which will serve as cues during your delivery.

It can be very difficult to relinquish sheaves of paper which hold previous, well-researched information in exchange for small rectangles of cardboard holding no more than a few headings. You may think you will never remember anything from them and the first time you attempt to rehearse your speech, your confidence can take a nose dive as you realize your worst fears.

This can be the danger period: the transition from paper to card – that reluctant surrendering of reassuring sheaves of rustling A4s. Try to see this as a testing time and, if you can, persevere and use the cards. Once you make that breakthrough you will go from strength to strength.

Reading a speech from paper can work if you are a well-practised speaker with the knack of being able to read aloud with an easy relaxed manner. But I think that in some ways this isharder than using cards. You need to recover your place on the sheet time and time again; the turning of the pages needs to be unobtrusive; and the contact with your audience is much more difficult to maintain when there is the written word separating the listeners from you. For people who have to make many presentations, reading may be the only practical solution, but generally, using cards is recommended.

Preparing prompt cards

If you decide to adopt the card method, here are some suggestions for layout:

1 Use one side of the card only.

2 Number each one clearly with a black or coloured pen.

3 List major points that need addressing but resist the temptation to cram more than the essentials on to the postcard, otherwise you may spend much of the speech with head bent, peering at details that have been written in tiny handwriting.

4 Any vital information that needs careful reference will need to be inserted for accuracy.

5 The cards may be separate or strung together, whichever is more comfortable.

Once you have done this, *practise*. That way you will improve and gain confidence. You will be able to look at the audience while you speak and communication will be at its strongest.

Rehearsing your speech

Familiarity breeds content! Once your notes have been pruned to postcard headings, rehearse your speech as often as you feel the need. (Chapter Three gives details about modulation skills to help your delivery.) Become familiar with your voice by monitoring it on a tape-recorder. This way you will receive quick, efficient feedback, and any improvements needed can be put into effect.

Tips for preparing a speech to read

1 Use a black pen on white paper and keep the writing quite large.

2 Rewrite your second draft in phrases and group them by ideas or in pairs.

3 Provide a good space between each phrase. This avoids confusion and marks the end of one idea and the beginning of another.

Writing out your speech in this way enables you to look at the audience regularly and then return to your place with comparative ease.

4 Write as you would speak and avoid the use of too many abstract concepts. Use pictorial language when the opportunity presents itself.

As mentioned earlier (see page 40), it is best to avoid the temptation of memorizing a speech. Some people will wish to do this as a back-up. However, it is much easier to forget *lines* than to forget the *gist* of what you wish to say. Forgetting a word or sentence can throw some people and thus undermine their confidence still further. Familiarizing is better than memorizing. It allows the speaker's personality to come into sharper focus and the speech will sound more spontaneous than word-by-word rendering.

So, make a friend of your speech and have fun rehearsing! Remember that the key word is *practise*!

Summary of planning your material

1 Begin research well in advance.

2 Research facts to ensure accuracy.

3 Avoid overloading with excessive amounts of information. Cut unnecessary padding. Aim to be economical.

4 Look for places where you can add light relief. (Jokes, quotations and definitions can be found in Chapters Seven, Eight and Nine.)

5 Be listener-orientated. Write to speak.

6 Be simple and direct by speaking in language the audience understands.

7 Write under four or five headings and, if necessary, sub-headings.

8 Have a clear, energetic and purposeful introduction.

9 Use reiteration where necessary, particularly in the summing up.

10 Write several drafts so that you can edit and re-edit.

11 Transfer the main points of your speech to cards, or rewrite the draft in phrases.

12 Mark where visual aids will be introduced.

13 Time the speech.

14 PRACTISE.

Speaking off the cuff

For those well versed in the art of public speaking this may not be difficult; for the novice it can be nerve-racking. My advice is always be prepared for the unexpected. If you attend a number of social functions and think that you might at some stage be asked to 'fill in' (give a vote of thanks or a talk, or introduce a speaker), carry with you a blueprint or skeleton speech (with the key points on cards) that can be used in an emergency. This is particularly appropriate if you think that you are not good at thinking on your feet.

Keep a notebook of amusing jokes and anecdotes (see Chapter Seven for ideas) and practise rehearsing one or two of these from time to time. This will help keep you on form and prepare you for that unexpected invitation.

3

PREPARING AND PRACTISING YOUR DELIVERY

The better your delivery, the better your speech. If you get your delivery perfected, your speech, whether for social or business, will have impact.

Modulation

Modulation is the use of expressive delivery. It can be thought of as having four elements: pause, pace, power and pitch.

Pause

The effective use of the pause

Before you start to speak, stop! Here's why:

1 A pause establishes your presence.

2 It gives you status.

3 The audience has time to look you over.

4 It gives them a chance to settle down.

5 It gives you a chance to be heard from word one!

If you begin your speech immediately, without waiting for complete quiet, you lose impact. Impact is vital!

Pause between paragraphs and changes of thought. This aids clarity and helps the audience absorb what has been said.

Pause and emphasis

While it is valuable to lay stress on principal words, raising the volume to add weight may not necessarily prove very effective. Here are some techniques that may be used to give emphasis, along with the pause.

Exercise 26 Pause and emphasis

The strokes indicate where you may pause. Highlighted words are in italics.

1 Pausing before and after the highlighted word:
The rain in Spain falls / *mainly* / **on the plain.**

2 You can bring down the volume and speak more slowly on the phrase you wish to emphasize:
The rain in Spain falls / *mainly on the plain.*

('Mainly on the plain' is spoken more quietly than the rest of the sentence.)

3 You can slightly elongate the highlighted word for emphasis. In this instance you may not wish to use pause:
The rain in Spain falls *m-a-i-n-l-y on the plain.*

Pronouns and adverbs are emphasized in cases of comparisons. Avoid over-emphasis when using conjunctions, articles, prepositions and subordinate words. For example:

Incorrect emphasis

In the beginning *was* the Word, and the Word was *with* God. And the Word *was* God.

Suggested emphasis

In the beginning was the *Word*, and the Word was with *God*. And the Word was *God*. (St John, Chapter 1)

Language needs to flow. If you speak it rhythmically, the sounds and messages will fall happily on the ears of listeners. Be selective when emphasizing words or statements and remember:
   'I PAUSE AND I THINK.'
   'I PAUSE AND YOU THINK.'

Words lead from thoughts! Relate sincerely with your audience. Let them see that you care about what you are saying. Allow your own personality to shine through. While you pause to think, the audience has space to process what has been said.

However, while natural use of both pause and emphasis is effective, remember that the over-use of both can be boring and affected.

Pace

It is important to regulate the passage of your speech. Avoid the tendency to speak at one rate throughout, either too fast or too slow. Never rush!

Pace is varied rate. It is the adjustment or words and phrases within the context of a speech. Consequently pace is closely linked with pause.

Remember to:

1 Breathe easily from your centre to help alleviate tension.

2 Use pauses between sentences and paragraphs and for effect.

Exercise 27 Monitoring the pace

Practise reading passages from a book or magazine. Listen to yourself on a tape-recorder to help you monitor your pace. Look for places where it can be varied. Ask yourself these questions:

1 What is the mood of the passage?

2 At what points should I slow down or speed up and why? Is it to:

Clarify a point or statement – slow down?

Help build a state of suspense – start slowly and then gain momentum by speeding up?

Pass over the less important features of the speech – speed up?

3 Am I speaking clearly in the faster passages?

Mood is a very important ingredient. Like the weather and temperature, it can change. Use those changes to add excitement, colour and depth to your work.

Power

Power is the volume, the energy behind the voice. It is the reinforcement of sound.

This is made possible by the use of the resonators and the breathing muscles. If we allow our outgoing breath to pass over the vocal chords in a positive, well-directed and steady stream of air, we can enlarge our sound. The more air pressure produced when breathing out, the louder the sound will be.

When you speak to an audience, the amount of power you need in your voice will depend on the size and acoustics of the room or hall. It is useful therefore to know beforehand about the venue. (See also Chapter Four.)

Remember that as you do the following exercise you will require good postural alignment, so that there is physical support and space in the throat and chest for breath. To help achieve this, place your hand on the midriff, and imagine sound as well as breath coming from your middle. This will enable your throat to feel free and open. Focus on what you are saying, and open your mouth for the words. This will help energize the sound and power of your voice. Aim for fullness of tone. Avoid shouting or straining from the throat.

Exercise 28 Power and projection 1

Using your largest room, choose an object near to you and make that your focal point. Speak the following sentence quietly and distinctly:

My message is clear.

Now move away from this point a couple of paces and repeat the sentence, slightly increasing your volume.

My message is clear.

When you are some distance from your starting point, change your sentence to:

My message is loud and clear.

Exercise 29 Power and projection 2

Now do the same with the following:

Good morning, everyone.

I call the meeting to order.

Quiet, ladies and gentlemen! The play is about to begin.

Timber!

Exercise 30 Varying the volume

Vary your voice according to the content of the following passage. Clarity of speech is vital, particularly when speaking the quieter portions. Avoid a fading-out of the voice.

The house you visit is a house of history. So pause awhile in our great hall. Absorb the atmosphere and quiet of this place.

Now view the tapestry; admire the craft. A needlework measured out in tiny stitches, which when completed tells of one enormous, bloody war. See, compacted in this weave, how combat sought political resolve.

Pitch

Pitch is the key in which we speak. In speech there are high, middle and low pitches.

When we speak, our various pitches tend to merge into one another and are dependent on the mood and the meaning of our speech. This is illustrated as follows:

High pitch

This is used in moments of exhilaration, excitement or happiness.

Middle pitch

This is used for general conversation and moderate speech.

Low pitch

This is used for sad and solemn speech.

Exercise and vary your pitch. It will enhance vocal expression and augment platform presence. Practise reading a fairy tale aloud. Imagine you have children as your audience. Make use of pause, emphasis, pace, volume and intensity. Decide the various moods of the passage and foster the different pitches to suit them.

Remember that with each new paragraph, the voice needs to be refreshed; so raise your pitch at the beginning slightly. This revives interest.

Intensity

Intensity is the pizzazz, the zing, zip, wallop of your speech! It is the sparkle behind your voice. Intensity is the life force – the energy and enthusiasm you inject into your manner and voice.

Vocally, it includes pause and emphasis, pace, pitch and power, with the added ingredients of sincerity, humour and goodwill.

Spiritually, it includes belief in your message and total involvement. So:

ATTACK YOUR SPEECH WITH ANIMATION AND DRIVE!

Give your audience mental shocks

While a speaker may appear to have a few fascinated listeners gazing up at the platform, this is not in itself proof that the listeners are riveted by his or her utterances! An attentive face may be concealing completely different thoughts: perhaps puzzling over the next meeting at the office, or whether or not they had remembered to lock the back door!

By stimulating the audience through modulation, the speaker keeps them alert. They will not have time to be distracted.

Passages for speaking practice

The following passages are for practice. Before you read them aloud, look again at:

Mood

The mood of a passage helps determine the way in which it is delivered. It is therefore important to establish this at the outset.

Breath Pauses

Go through a passage and mark breaks for supplementary breaths, at full stops and ends of paragraphs.

Pace

Look for where the pace might be varied. Be guided by content.

Pitch

Vary the key of your voice in accordance with mood and material.

Emphasis

Stress important words, those used to make a comparison, and words that add colour. Avoid being too emphatic, as this can destroy the flow.

Power and intensity

The volume of a passage will be dependent on mood. Increasing power by degrees can help build a feeling of suspense and climax. Speaking quietly can also create atmosphere, and is a most effective way of highlighting important material. Remember to speak with energy and involvement.

Pause

Having established where you are going to take your breaks at full stops, some commas, between paragraphs and with changes of thought, there may also be places where pause can be used to create effect. Knowing how long to pause develops with experience. Never milk a pause for its own sake but rather use with discretion – mindful of the needs of your audience.

FRIENDS

Harry Trafford rushed onto the platform just as his train drew out of the little country station. He watched its snake-like course, as it gradually disappeared from view. Resignedly, Harry put his suitcase down and sat on it. He shivered. This was not the kind of weather to hang about outside.

For some time Harry sat there, trying to ignore the sharp February chill that furtively seeped through his body. He gave an involuntary shudder – the next train was not due for another two hours. What on earth was he to do in the meantime? Apart from the station master, the place was deserted. It was then he heard footsteps behind him. They stopped just by his suitcase. Harry viewed a very expensive pair of brogues.

'Harry! Harry Trafford! What on earth are you doing in this neck of the woods?'

Harry looked up from his low vantage point and saw the familiar corpulence of his old university mate.

'Ken? I can't believe it! Of all the places to bump into you!' Harry jumped to his feet, and grasped Ken by the hand. His face beamed. Ken laughed. 'I just live round the corner. Dropped by to book my ticket to town for tomorrow morning. Thought I'd avoid the rush! Believe it or not, we're quite busy here early mornings – commuters, you know. Look, there's my local across the road. Shall we go and sink a few pints for old times' sake?'

Harry picked up his case. 'Let's do just that!'

THE HAT BOX

Travelling on the underground
From Waterloo to Charing Cross.
Directly opposite me
A woman sits,
With hat box
Resting on her knee.

Inscrutable – expressionless
She stares ahead, a world apart.
Hand gently rests upon her charge,
Black striped box
Bound with string,
Hexagonal and large.

Perhaps her wedding veil it holds,
Or picture hat in white tissue.
A dimpled grotto of delight,
Shop-smelling, luscious, new.

At Charing Cross we leave the train
To go our separate ways.
She with hat box held aloft,
And I go home to Hayes.

THE CLOCK

The Victorian grandfather clock stopped at 4 a.m. on the 21st of November, 1965. It stopped the moment that Richard's father died. He would've liked to have sold it then, discharged himself of its painful associations, but could not bring himself to do so. Instead, he compromised by not resetting the hands.

The clock now stood estranged, gathering dust in a darkened corner of the landing. When Richard went to bed, he sometimes forgot to switch on the upstairs lights, and occasionally fancied that the grandfather clock took on the appearance of a person standing in shadow; standing and waiting.

Then, on the first anniversary of his father's death, at 4 a.m. precisely, the clock struck the hour. It resounded almost defiantly throughout the large house. The insistent chimes penetrated Richard's dream. He started awake and rushed out of his bedroom and onto the landing, shaking from the fright that comes with interrupted sleep, but the last note was now dying on the air. The clock nursed its seal of secrecy.

Richard didn't sleep again that night, and next morning he restarted the clock. He reset the hands and wound it with the key his father had used. Listening to the old familiar tick, he felt surprisingly reassured. He polished the wood and some of its former glory was restored, although it was still darkened by sooty shadow. Richard switched on the landing light. It was as though he saw the clock for the first time. He smiled: 'I hadn't noticed before what a handsome face you have.' (His father had been handsome.) 'I think I'll go out this morning and buy a spotlight. You need to be seen, old chap! Now why didn't I think of that before?'

Speaking dialogue

Use this passage to practise dialogue. Vary your pitch level to establish the different characters. The mood needs to be light and the dialogue quick on cues. Keep up the pace and discover where you can use pause to good effect.

LOVE'S TREASURE

Henry Price, romantic novelist, living on the outskirts of Weston-super-Mare, opened the front door of his house one morning last June, and found himself face to face with the beautiful Angela Culpepper.

'I've come about the job.'

'Job?'

'Yes, your advert – in the paper. I rang – you asked me to come.'

'Oh yes. Yes, of course. Miss er...'

'Culpepper. But you can call me Angela if you like.'

'Follow me, Angela, and turn right. Mind the step. Here we are. This is the study where I work. A bit cramped, I'm afraid – never managed to acquire a decent one. Take a seat, won't you? I'll just move these papers – clear the decks so to speak. Oh, get off there, you stupid animal – Shoo! Out you go!' A tortoiseshell cat leapt off a pile of books, causing a lamp shade to sway precariously on its stand.

'Now then, I'd like to take one or two details if I may. I'll just get my notebook if I can find it under all the paperwork.'

'Here's your notebook.' Angela's smile as she handed it to him so fascinated Henry, that he could only stare. She couldn't be more than twenty-four or so, he thought. Tall, slim, skin the colour of ivory, milky-blue eyes, chestnut hair that caught the light when she moved her head. Oh, but she was lovely. Yes, he could see her fitting perfectly into his next novel.

Creating beautiful women was part of Henry's job as a writer. In the past it had afforded him a great deal of pleasure. Now, at sixty-four, his inventive powers were beginning to wane and while his income allowed him and his wife to live out their days in relative comfort, Henry needed fresh stimulus to revive his old writing skills.

'Anything the matter, Mr Price?'

'No, no, it was nothing, nothing at all. Well, as you may know, I'm an author. Have you heard of me?' Henry shot Angela an uncertain glance.

'No, I don't read very much.'

'Ah well, no matter. I write romantic fiction. At present I'm in the process of finishing the final draft of *Love's Treasure*. Now what I need is someone such as yourself to type the manuscript for me. Not too worried about speed, but must be accurate, you understand. You do touch-type?'

'Yes.'

'Good, very good.' (Those eyes! He must concentrate, damn it.)

'Cash in hand as advertised – flexi-hours – two or three

mornings a week. Will you accept the job?' Henry held his breath.

'Yes. Thank you very much. I'd like to accept.'

'Next Monday suit you?'

'Yes.'

'Then Monday it is.'

'Freda,' he said to his wife later that morning, 'she's perfect, quite perfect.'

4

GIVING YOUR PRESENTATION

Your speech has been written, your cards are prepared, your visual aids, if you are using them (see Chapter Five), are assembled. It is now useful to acquire some information about the place in which you are to speak.

Communicate with the programme organizer

Whether this is a social or business occasion, here are some questions you might ask:

1 How many people will be in the audience?

2 How many speakers are there going to be?

3 How long should my speech last?

4 Will the chairperson or organizer write a brief initial introduction about me, or should I prepare one beforehand?

5 What is the size of the room in which I will speak?

6 Will I be required to speak at a lectern?

7 Will there be a microphone? A projector?

8 Will I be standing on a raised platform or on a level with the audience?

Know the venue and the seating arrangements

If the room is large and the seats arranged in theatre style, you will need to throw your voice to the back of the hall. Acoustics will also affect carrying power. So, if there is an opportunity, practise a few sentences for sound level before the event. If speaking to a very large audience for any length of time, some form of amplification will be required. When the room is arranged horseshoe fashion, the audience will be much smaller: fifteen to twenty people. This can be an ideal setting, because it encourages rapport within the group. Also the speaker can move easily among them.

Request your needs

If you are the sole speaker, politely expressing your wishes will help you to prepare with confidence. For example, if it is to be a small grouped audience and you like the idea of arranging the seats in a horseshoe fashion, send in a diagram suggesting this.

Will you be introduced?

If there is a chairperson in charge, ask whether or not you as the speaker will be introduced to the audience. As a good deal of time and effort will have gone into the talk, you will deserve a decent build-up!

You may like to write your own initial introduction and send it ahead to the chairperson. Give some local background on yourself: your achievements and interests. Keep it short.

If you are to be introduced, you may wish to thank the person who has introduced you, or acknowledge certain people present (the chairperson or president and the audience) before beginning your speech.

Take time for a dress rehearsal

If possible arrive early so that you can check on the following:

The lighting

A speaker needs to be well lit on all sides. Make sure there will not be lights shining into your eyes.

The microphone

For rooms and small halls the natural voice can be used. But generally, in large halls, especially those that are acoustically poor, some form of amplification will be necessary. Will the microphone be fixed or hand-held, or will you wear it on you? Consider the following tips when using a microphone.

1 Modulate the movement of the head with the amplitude of the voice. Remember that close up, a small movement away from the microphone can mean a large drop in volume. So when speaking normally, keep close up to it.

2 If the microphone has only a small windshield, keep the head about four inches away from it. Speak out to avoid 'popping'.

3 If using a tie-clip microphone, clip it as close to the mouth as possible and speak out.

4 When holding a microphone, avoid 'handling noise'.

Gestures

Be economical with these. Too many can be a source of distraction. If you will be holding cards or notes, practise beforehand the gestures you wish to make.

Remember:

1 The gesture slightly precedes the word.

2 Try not to lean while making gestures.

3 Keep eyes raised.

4 Arm movements should be large enough to be seen. Make them from the waist with firmness and flow.

The use of gestures

Gestures made in the course of everyday life are natural, spontaneous movements, expressing an attitude of mind. They may arise from emotional feeling, or they may be used to express an idea, illustrate a point, or reinforce an argument.

Unfortunately when we are on show, either acting or giving a speech, our dialogue, however well intended or felt, is not entirely natural. It has been rehearsed. In addition, we can become acutely self-aware and, while consciousness of self is essential, overt self-consciousness can result in tensions which promote graceless, staccato movements and gestures, undermining the speaker and acting as a distraction.

Discipline your gestures by learning to stand or sit still. It is irritating to watch a speaker sway from side to side, or pace up and down on a platform like a trapped animal. Initially and most importantly, learn the art of repose. If while making a speech, you are using cards on which are written key points, hold these just below chest level so that you are able to look at your audience, and speak out. This has now given you something to do with your hands. If you need to use an arm movement, your right or left hand is available to do so. Stand with your legs slightly apart, with the weightevenly distributed on both feet. This 'grounds' you, and may act as a reminder to keep still.

The use of too many gestures can be distracting, however well thought out, so use these economically. Let your thoughts guide your movements, and remember that they need to be allied with facial and vocal expression.

Avoiding irritating habits

Repetitive movements or sounds are thrown into high relief when speaking in front of a group of people. Some habits to avoid are:

'Uhhs' and 'Uhmms'

Short coughs or sniffs

Smacking the lips

Biting the lips

Touching the ear or nose

Repeated adjustment of spectacles

Scratching the head

Fiddling with necktie or necklace

Swaying from side to side

Pacing up and down like an animal in captivity

Looking downwards too much instead of at the audience

Asking someone to video you will probably seem very daunting, but if you get the chance you will be able to monitor any habits.

What should I do with my hands?

If you are using prompt cards, hold these with both hands, just below chest level. As described above, when you want to make a gesture, your right or left hand can be used. Holding your cards in this way looks good and prevents unnecessary fidgeting. Avoid placing one hand in your pocket while holding the cards in the other: it looks slovenly and, particularly for the business environment, unprofessional.

When cards are not being used, avoid crossing your arms but adopt a position that is comfortable for you. For example, one arm may rest in front of you at waist level, and the other down at your side. Later, during your speech, the two arms can remain at your side. Alternatively, your arms may be placed in front of you, one hand resting on the other. Some people like to stand with their arms held behind their back. All these postures are acceptable, but varying them throughout your speech will create a more relaxed and confident look.

Checking your appearance

Aim at being comfortable and smart. Fashion is changing all the time, so the suggestions given here are guidelines only:

For the woman

As the main source of focus will be on the face, pay special attention to make-up if you wear it. Strong lighting drains natural colour, so it's a good idea to apply blusher and emphasize the lips and the eyes.

Keep the hair away from the face, so that it is not masked, but retain a soft style.

Earrings can soften the face and add interest, but avoid the large, dangling variety: they will be a distraction.

A colourful scarf or brooch adds a touch of sophistication and interest to the neckline.

Avoid wearing dull colours unless they are offset by something bright and cheerful, such as a scarf. Red is a strong, dramatic hue, and providing it doesn't drain colour from the face, can create impact. Avoid busy patterns. They are too tiring on the eye.

Check that your hemlines are straight, especially if wearing a full skirt, as these sometimes have a tendency to dip.

For the man

Wear a well-fitting suit and shirt with the cuffs just showing below the jacket. The tie should be neatly tied.

Black shoes are preferable to brown: brown tends to distract the eye. Dark-coloured socks should be worn, rather than white. Make sure the socks cover the calves adequately.

For the less formal occasion, smart casual may be worn.

Smile please!

Even, white teeth are a cosmetic asset to the platform speaker, but not everyone is blessed with a perfect set of these. Some speakers are afraid to smile, because of being self-conscious of their imperfect teeth. The hand goes up to the mouth, or the expression remains solemn in order to hide the teeth. If this is the case with you, in addition to making your own routine check-ups, either get your teeth fixed by the dentist, or make up your mind to forget about them, and be yourself. The confident person will smile anyway!

How are you feeling?

Nervous reactions can inhibit hunger pangs, so that while we may not experience a desire for food, our stomachs may tell us otherwise and protest by rumbling. This can be a source of personal embarrassment. If you think this may happen to you, eat a little food containing complex carbohydrate, such as a fresh banana (not over-ripe) or nuts, prior to your speech appointment. This will also help give you some energy.

If this is an after-dinner speech, or another social occasion, monitor your alcohol consumption throughout the meal or celebration. There is nothing more embarrassing (and indeed insulting to your host or guest of honour) than a drunken, slurred speaker. From your own point of view, even being slightly tipsy, particularly if you've never spoken in public before, will make you feel less in control and lacking in confidence.

Last minute tips

Listen while you wait

If you are one of several speakers waiting their turn, focus on every word that your fellow speakers are saying. It rehearses your powers of concentration and temporarily directs attention away from yourself. This may help alleviate feelings of nervousness.

Speak out

When using prompt cards or sheets of paper for notes, ensure they are held just below chest level. Any lower and the neck bends too far, causing the voice to direct itself to the floor. Speak directly to your listeners.

Quietly does it

Before giving a speech for a social occasion, leave yourself plenty of time on the day to prepare. You may like to rehearse your speech once more, and then save your voice as much as possible. Conserve your energy and you will remain calmer than if you rush about or engage in a good deal of unnecessary chat. Save social talk for the event in hand and avoid wearing yourself out before making your speech.

Summary of points to check before the speech

1 *Give yourself permission to feel nervous!* The time to get worried is when you are not! Use feelings of nervousness positively, to propel you into action. This will give you the energy and drive needed to deliver a strong, animated speech.

2 *Use relaxation and breathing exercises.* This will help keep feelings of nervousness under control. Correct breathing will also help support the voice.

3 *Be gentle with yourself.* Be generous with self-praise. Criticize yourself constructively, not destructively. Remember that practice makes for improvement.

4 *Observe and listen.* Learn your craft by listening to other good speakers and observing their style and delivery.

5 *Keep the voice well oiled!* Practise vocal exercises to improve quality, range and clarity. Remember to think of sound as coming from your middle.

6 *Look forward!* Prepare well in advance. More delay, more dread!

Condition your mind to look forward to the event. Imagine how you would feel if, after all your hard homework, the speech was cancelled at the last minute.

7 *'With all good wishes for a happy speech.'* Greet your audience with pleasure. Let them see through your animated language and expression that you are glad to be there.

8 *Give yourself a 'facial'.* Practise facial exercises to tone the muscles and help you relax. Rehearse speaking in warm tones. Imagine giving a talk on the radio. Use a 'vocal smile' to express yourself.

9 *Physical awareness.* Easy, relaxed bearing will help promote a feeling of well-being. It will transmit to the audience an air of confidence. Release tension in the shoulders and neck by practising Exercises 2, 3 and 4 in Chapter One.

10 *Irritating habits.* Try asking a close friend to tell you what yours are – a test of real friendship!

11 *Appearance.* Wear clothes that are comfortable, but smart. Choose colours and styles that are flattering and provide some interest; for example, an arresting tie for the man, an unusual scarf for the woman.

12 *Arrive in good time.* If you have been able to liaise with the programme organizer you will know whether or not you can run through a few last-minute preparations such as checking for lighting and sound.

13 *Be prepared.* If this is a business presentation or a talk to a local society or group, will there be a 'Question Time' at the end of the evening?

When you walk onto the platform ...

Make a good first impression

If walking to a platform, adopt an easy gait. Arms swinging naturally; body straight.

Give your audience your best wishes from word one. Show them that you are happy to be there, by wearing a relaxed warm expression. It is easy and understandable to appear stern-faced when nervous. The facial muscles can get tight. Practising a few mouth, lip and tongue exercises beforehand can help. (See Chapter One.)

Animate your body movements

The audience needs a sense of direction, a feeling that the speaker is in charge and can be trusted. Positive body language can help achieve this.

If using a lectern, place your notes on it with a quick glance down, and then look at your audience. Remember to keep the eyes up as much as possible and certainly during the introduction, when you should be looking at the audience.

Smile as you speak

Smile as you make your opening remarks. This is a very difficult thing to do, but necessary. Thereafter use dimpling of the face. Imagine having a face lift! The cheeks and lips are slightly raised, as though you are about to smile. This way you appear more approachable and attractive.

Focusing on your audience

When there is a large audience present, it is sometimes difficult to know where to look when making a speech. If there is strong stage lighting, it is unlikely that you will be able to see your audience, in which case, individual eye contact is impossible. If there is a central exit light at the back of the hall, use that as your main focus point. In between times the eyes can travel to the right-hand side of the hall and then the left, always homing back to the exit sign. This gives the illusion of looking at your audience.

Jokes

Make sure the jokes of your speech are acceptable to the audience.

Don't risk offending or embarrassing anyone. Refer to Chapter Seven for detailed advice on using jokes appropriately.

Accepting compliments

Some people find it hard to accept compliments. They feel uncomfortable, become self-effacing and embarrassed. Unused to praise, they dismiss, deny or overlook the giver's good opinion. These are negative and rejecting responses to compliments that have been given in good faith. Pleased to receive them, confident speakers will courteously respond to plaudits by accepting them with grace and charm.

If you are commended, return the compliment by accepting it. Retain eye contact with the giver and express your gratitude with warmth and sincerity. A simple 'Thank you' or 'Thank you, I appreciate that' can be sufficient.

Taking the chair

An effective chairperson is rather like a good parent. He or she casts a caring eye over their charge without interfering on all fronts. They allow events to develop democratically, without denying the right of self-expression and freedom. They are firm without being authoritarian and crushing in their role, and they see that there is fair play.

If you consider becoming a chairperson, ask yourself these questions:

1 Have I got leadership skills?

2 How do I function in a group setting?

3 Am I patient?

4 Am I assertive?

5 Do I possess a sense of fair play?

6 Am I methodical?

You will have some idea what your communication skills are like from past records at school and college, or at work. Of course, we don't always see ourselves as others view us, but we often have a pretty good idea. If you are unsure as to whether or not you are fitted for the job, pluck up courage and ask one or two good friends how you come across and encourage them to suggest areas where they think you could improve. For example, you may be assertive in some areas, but impatient or short-tempered in others. There are times when we may justify certain traits within ourselves, without stopping to re-evaluate our viewpoint. While you may not have taken a front-line position in the past, consider accepting an offer to take the chair.

The principal duties of the chairperson are to keep order, to deal with relevant business, to say who shall speak, and to put resolutions to the vote. The chairperson declares the opening and closing of meetings and is the general overseer of the proceedings. If there are speakers, they should always address the chairperson first before commencing their speech, often as Mr Chairman or Madam Chairwoman.

The chairperson will follow an agenda. This may include: a welcome and reasons for the meeting; apologies for absence; the minutes of the last meeting (which will have been taken down by the secretary); matters arising from the last meeting; reports (such as a treasurer's report); points that may arise from these reports; any other business; the date set for the next meeting.

Introducing a speaker

If you are introducing a speaker, do it with momentum. Here are some suggestions:

1 Say his or her name strongly, clearly and slowly. This gives the audience time to digest the information.

2 Introduce the person with enthusiasm and warmth.

3 Include him or her in your body language. Look at the person

briefly and turn yourself in their direction at least once. Practise swivelling your body round, using the feet as a pivot.

4 'Ladies and gentlemen, John Smith.' As you speak include an arm gesture at this point. Small movements look awkward and will not be seen at the back. Use a wide gesture and let it flow from the waist. Practise until this comes naturally.

5 Make sure that your voice does not drop when your body is turned away from the audience.

Thanking the speaker

If you make the introduction, it is important that you listen carefully to everything the speaker has to say. You can then include in your vote of thanks several points of interest that may have been made during the speech.

Avoid a eulogistic vote of thanks. This can be embarrassing for the speaker, and may not be in accordance with the views of the audience.

If the speech was poor, a polite but short vote of thanks will suffice. This avoids embarrassment all round, as the speaker may know his or her performance was weak, and any hypocrisy will most likely be detected.

Your vote of thanks can be formal or informal.

Summary of a chairperson's duties

As a chairperson, you will lead events, so remember:

1 Learn all the rules and procedures before starting out. Revise them thoroughly. Ensure that you are told about relevant issues that need addressing. The secretary deals with the minutes, but you should look at these prior to a meeting.

2 Arrive in good time to make any preparations.

3 Be firm but friendly.

4 Keep to the agenda and be succinct. Avoid straying from the point. Use interim summaries to help you and to guide members.

5 Deal kindly and encouragingly with those people who are shy speaking out in a group. Sometimes it is they who can contribute most.

6 Aim to foster a wide spread of opinions. Some people love to talk for talking's sake, and meetings can provide the perfect opportuny for this to happen. Be polite but firm. Suggest to them that someone else might like to express their view. If no one is forthcoming, continue to the next piece of business.

7 Be aware of the needs of those present. Meetings can be very protracted and boring, so keep up the pace but avoid rushing. Be firm, and guided by what is going on around you. Maintain good eye contact with those present.

8 As a chairperson, you may be expected to host visiting speakers. Ensure that they are made to feel comfortable. You may have liaised with them before their arrival. Ensure that the seating and microphones are arranged correctly and are suitable for the speaker's needs. If it is practically possible, let them acclimatize themselves to the setting in which they will speak.

9 Ensure that you know the speaker's names and that the pronunciation is correct, so that when you introduce them to the audience, you get it right.

10 You may know the length of the speech or speeches in advance, but it is an idea to double-check with those concerned, particularly if there are several talks taking place. This can pre-empt any future embarrassment should a speaker over-run his or her time.

11 If a speech does over-run or is exceptionally tedious, you can scribble a note signalling the speaker to wind up as soon as possible. You are justified in doing so, if you have indicated the time limit in advance.

12 At question time following a speech, questions may either go through you as chair, or be directly addressed to the speaker. If there is aggravation caused by an audience member you can intervene, but avoid unnecessary nannying. There is more advice about question and answer sessions in Chapter Five.

13 Remember to send a letter of thanks to a visiting speaker, and possible travelling expenses if required.

5

BUSINESS PRESENTATIONS AND AFTER-DINNER SPEAKING

The effectiveness of a business presentation, no matter how large or small the audience, is largely dependent on the manner in which it is delivered. A pleasing tonality of voice, use of emphasis, pause, pace and volume can enhance a presentation and greatly increase audience interest which may be of vital importance to those involved. To this end, it is imperative that you prepare yourself and your material well. Refer back to the previous chapters for help with coping with nerves, improving your voice control, personal presentation and the planning of your speech itself.

If you have been asked to make a business presentation, consider this checklist before you commence your planning:

1 Who will comprise my audience? Will they be all levels of employees, a small management team, or newcomers to the company?

2 Is the occasion formal or informal? (This will affect the style of speech as well as perhaps the clothing you choose to wear.)

3 Do the audience have any prior knowledge of the subject? (Refer back to Chapter Two for more advice about this.)

4 How many speakers are there? If there are others, establish with them what they plan to do on the day. (Refer to Chapter Four for advice about communicating with the programme organizer.)

5 Will you be introduced or will you be introducing yourself? (Again, see Chapter Four for guidelines on this.)

6 Will you be able to use visual aids? (There is advice on using visual aids on pages 74–5.)

7 Will there be a question and answer session at the end? (Refer to pages 75–6.)

8 Will you be preparing sheets and handouts to accompany your presentation?

Giving the presentation

As already stated, the advice given in the preparation and planning chapters of this book applies to all types of speeches and presentations. However, there are some particular points which you may wish to bear in mind for a business situation.

Hooking your audience

Audience interest will be at its height at the beginning of a speech. After that there is a tendency for concentration to flag, with occasional periods of increased interest. If the audience senses the end of a talk, it will revive itself, anxious not to miss any vital information. The renewed interest is not, however, as strong as the initial curiosity.

From this we may deduce that:

A strong introduction is important.

An energetic introduction is important.

Audiences desire strong direction.

So:

Clearly state the title of the presentation; e.g. 'Our topic is "Industry Today".'

Clearly state the headlines under which you will speak: 'I will deal with this topic under five main headings.'

The listeners will have been led and motivated into a more attentive frame of mind by a speaker who is specific and aware of the needs of the audience.

Breaking up the presentation

If the presentation is quite a long one, let your listeners know when you have reached the end of the first part of the talk. This guides them and revives their interest. At least one conclusion will be necessary. Draw all the links of your chain together and sum up the points that you have already made. As a speaker, you should keep bringing the audience back to your attention. Listeners need to receive small mental shocks from time to time, otherwise the whole thing can become woolly and vague in their memories.

Feedback

End by summarizing. Reiteration is important if the audience is to retain what has been said. The more technical the presentation, the greater the need for clarity.

Using visual aids

Your speech will often be more interesting and informative if the audience has something to look at. When planning the content, think about where you could bring in an illustration.

Keep visual aids as simple as possible. Your main contact is with the audience. Don't be tempted to hide behind visual aids – use them as an adjunct to, not a substitute for your speech.

Check the lighting equipment in the room and whether or not the main light works off a dimmer. This can be useful for showing slides.

If there is a programme organizer, it is important to know the set-up and have a chance to test out with the engineer for sound, light, etc.

Slides

Make sure that you keep the message simple on each slide. Code the slides for insertion and index them for correct sequence.

Use of a board

As it is difficult for an audience to digest too much information, very important material can be highlighted by writing on a board or overhead projector and articulating what is written. In certain instances you may need to repeat yourself.

Study sheets can be circulated or sent by post before the talk. Decide at which point(s) you are going to distribute them. Be careful that the listeners are not side-tracked or reading the sheets when you would like them to be listening to you.

The flip chart

This is useful with small audiences where everyone is near enough to see it clearly. It can help the talk to flow.

Three-dimensional objects

These are of particular interest to an audience. Think about how you are going to pass them round and collect them. Remember to give them time to take in what they are seeing. Avoid talking too much at this point as it can be distracting.

Any questions?

This is your chance to get positive feedback from the audience. If there is an efficient chairperson present, he or she will monitor the action. Alternatively, engage one or two friends or colleagues to set the ball rolling.

Have an idea in your mind of the type of questions you may be asked, including the tough ones. If you don't know the answer, say so and open it to the floor.

Prepare your answer as the question is being asked. Try to be one step ahead. Be as precise as possible.

If a question is asked too quietly, repeat it for the sake of the audience. Equally important, rephrase a question that has been poorly expressed.

Get an idea beforehand as to the length of the question time. When it is nearly over prepare your audience: 'I think we have time for two more questions.'

If there is an awkward customer in the audience, try to remain calm. If he or she is a persistent heckler, you can suggest that they stay behind afterwards to discuss the subject further. That gets rid of them temporarily and minimizes the disruption.

Encouraging listeners to write in their questions may prove a little dull and lacking in spontaneity.

If it is appropriate, you can throw in the odd question yourself. This can keep things going and add stimulus.

How did you do?

The following are some points to consider when assessing your speech or listening to others. You will inevitably be asked to speak again, and in the business environment it is best to use every opportunity for improvement. The Plus points are on the left, the Minuses on the right.

Personality

Confident	Uncertain
Authoritative	Unsure
Composed	Edgy
Lively	Dull
Warm	Cold
Good audience contact	Withdrawn
Good audience reaction	Failure to move audience

Good eye contact	Eyes directed away from audience
Fluent speech	Abrupt/disjointed
Appropriate humour	Unimaginative/boring in content
Appropriate gestures	Distracting/unnecessary gestures
Relaxed movement	Over-tense

Voice and speech

Clear enunciation	Unclear enunciation
Efficient breath control	Poor breath control
Adequate voice projection	Weak voice projection or over-loud
Variety of tone using pause, pace, power, pitch	Monotonous delivery

The introduction

Imaginative	Mundane

The development of the speech

Logical	Muddled
Economical	Disjointed/rambling
Clear stages of progression	Too protracted
Accuracy of facts	Inaccuracy of facts
Efficient use of language	Pedantic/difficult to understand/long-winded
Use of humour	Humourless
Keeping to time limit	Over-long
Appropriate use of emphasis to aid clarity	Lack of definition
Stages recapped and checked; use of interim as well as final summary	Insensitive to audience needs
Keeping to the point	Digressing
Aim and scope of speech given	Lack of direction/vague/poor format

Work-related parties

The office Christmas party will, of course, be a very relaxed affair and any speech given here should usually be humorous (without giving offence) and remain up-beat and congratulatory, thanking everyone for their commitment and contributions over the previous year. Any other personnel matters will include birthdays (see Chapter Six for more information about such celebrations), retirement, leaving parties and promotions. As a general rule, keep comments positive, light-hearted but well intentioned and well-researched.

After-dinner speaking

A person is invited to give an after-dinner speech because he or she is either well known in a particular field, someone of high repute, or renowned for after-dinner speaking. To receive such an invitation is an honour that should not be taken lightly.

You should take care in the preparation of your speech and make absolutely certain that it runs for the time required, is relevant and entertaining. As a rule, an after-dinner speech is longer than any of the other speeches (rather than presentations) mentioned in this book. But the basic rules of preparation and delivery covered in the earlier chapters still prevail. If you are in doubt refer back to them.

If you are likely to be called upon as a regular after-dinner speaker, or if you decide to take it up as a paying proposition, you will need to keep a fund of anecdotes relative to your chosen subject. If these anecdotes relate to your own personal experiences so much the better. Refer to Chapters Seven, Eight and Nine for useful material to entertain your audience with.

6

WEDDINGS AND OTHER CELEBRATIONS

Of course, the same basic rules of speech writing and delivery apply to weddings as well as any other social occasions but there are some more specific things that you should bear in mind. When first sitting down to write your speech it may be a good idea to ask yourself why you have been asked to speak? Is it because you are expected to express good wishes or thanks, or because you are old and wise and expected to give advice, or because you are an extrovert and known for being humorous, because you are closely related to the other members of the family, or because you are a friend who has known the bride and groom for many years? The answer to this question may suggest to you what sort of speech to give. (Remember to consider carefully how long you will speak for: as a rule of thumb, if the occasion is a very formal one it will demand a longer speech.)

Whatever the cause of celebration, you will need to 'do your homework' if your speech is not only going to be amusing and clearly delivered, but relevant to the people present.

Gathering information

Before even attempting to write your speech, take stock of the information you have to hand and see where the gaps occur. Only then should you set about researching in order to fill your speech out, make it interesting, witty, or whatever style of speech you would like to make.

Begin your research by looking for ideas on which you can expound and expand. For instance, the theme of marriage itself is always popular. You could research ideas on the history of marriage and interesting marriage customs both here and abroad.

In addition you could ask the parents of the bride and groom about their marriages (checking on any divorces and remarriages to avoid embarrassment later) Enquire about the cake, photographer, transport, food, music, dancing, honeymoon destination, and first home. The living grandparents, uncles and aunts may also have interesting stories about their weddings, and marriages of friends, brothers, sisters and other relatives which took place in unusual or typically different circumstances in earlier days. Very often the best time to get people to talk about themselves is when you are sitting around the table over a meal or having tea, and when they are relaxed and are not likely to be diverted by other activities.

From the family history you can learn about the family's ancestors, where they have lived and worked and where they met, their education, work skills, achievements, hobbies and characters. Personal anecdotes can be added. You will need to strike a balance between personal and general remarks. It would be unfortunate if you generalized a great deal and delivered a speech which could have been given at anybody's wedding, when the bride and groom have fascinating family histories.

Make enquiries from both sides of the family. The discovery of the meaning of the family name may be news to the other side. And the countries all the grandparents came from could be quite interesting. But so is the fact that one or both families have lived in the same area for four generations. This is not the sort of information which would make the front pages of a newspaper, but you can assume that on the day everyone will be interested in the bride and groom and their respective families. The profession of the bride or groom may also provide speech matter.

Work out the structure

There is detailed information in Chapter Two about how you should set about writing your speech but for a wedding or other family occasion, you should pay particular attention to avoiding any stereotyped ideas and ensure that you delete anything that is in dubious taste – if in doubt, leave it out. Avoid negatives, regrets, criticisms of others, making the families appear foolish, making yourself appear foolish, and anything vague.

Remove rude jokes and deliberate sexist and sexual innuendos, and also watch out for unintended double entendres which might make inebriated members of the audience laugh when you are being serious and sincere.

Try to anticipate any controversial subjects and disasters you might have to mention, or avoid mentioning, in the course of your speech. Make yourself a troubleshooter's checklist. What would I say if: her father died; his parents couldn't attend; her parents didn't attend; the best man didn't arrive because his plane from India was delayed; it turned out to be the groom's second wedding, although it is her first; the Matron of Honour didn't turn up because she was ill; the groom dried up and forgot to compliment the bridesmaids so I couldn't thank him?

You may also have to state facts which are obvious to you, but not to cousins who have not seen the family for several years. You might also have to avoid stating the obvious. If this is to be a formal wedding, establish if there are any forms of address and particular titles which should be used for important personages. If there are, look these up in a suitable reference book.

For a transatlantic wedding, eliminate any Americanisms and

consider making jokes about the differences between Americanisms and conventional English language. If in doubt about anything, look it up in a dictionary of American expressions.

Finally, try to check that your speech will fit in with the speeches and toasts which will be given by others. Be sure that you know the name of the previous speaker so that you can say 'Thank you, George,' confident that his name is not James. And if one of the people you are speaking about is usually called 'Al', on this occasion should you be calling him by his full name (and if so, is that Albert, Alfred, Ali, Alexis, Alexander) or, even more formally, Mr Smith?

The delivery

The rules of diction, voice control and general performance (see Chapters One, Three and Four) will apply to anyone giving a speech at a wedding. When you rehearse your speech, you should also consider some changes in emotion: gratitude, surprise, amusement and seriousness. Decide what is the most important word in the sentence. Should the sentence, 'I have never seen such a beautiful bride' be read as, 'I have NEVER seen such a beautiful bride', or 'I have never seen such a BEAUTIFUL bride'? Underline any key phrases or words in your speech cards or notes. Your facial expressions can help to emphasize parts of your speech too: try smiling, scowling, or raising your eyebrows. If you will be expected to use a microphone, refer to the advice given in Chapter Four.

If you are speaking at the end of a meal, pace your alcohol consumption carefully – it would not only be personally embarrassing to be too drunk to speak but could cause offence to the bridal party. If you've been asked to propose a toast, stand and rehearse this in front of a full-length mirror, checking that you are smiling and making the right gestures, including lifting your glass sufficiently high and forward to convey enthusiasm.

And finally, remember that you won't be talking to a crowd

of strangers, but a crowd of friends. Your audience will not be critical – they want you to succeed and you can rely on their good-will. Look at people and smile at them. This is a happy occasion and a party occasion so almost certainly they will be smiling back!

Wedding etiquette

The purpose of etiquette is to provide an easy set of rules which we can follow when we are in a hurry and want to make sure that we do not give offence to anybody. The rules are most useful on formal occasions like weddings, and particularly when they happen only once in a lifetime. But because lifestyles are changing constantly the rules of etiquette are changing too.

The timing of speeches and toasts

Circumstances and ideas vary in different countries and the rules of speechmaking differ for different religions. When speeches are made after seated dinners at lengthy, formal wedding receptions, they begin after all eating at the formal meal has finished, and are preceded by the announcement from the toastmaster, 'Ladies and Gentlemen, you may now smoke'. If the meal finishes with tea or coffee and wedding cake, speeches will be made after the cutting of the cake. There is a natural tendency to call for speeches after the bride and groom have stood behind the cake to be photographed. It is easier to hold the attention of the diners at the end of the meal while they are seated, and still too full to want to get up and start dancing.

However, if the celebration is to continue all evening and the tea and coffee and wedding cake are to be served later, it is possible to delay the cutting of the cake until after the speeches which conclude the meal. Whatever the wedding organizers decide, it is important to let the toastmasters and the speechmakers know, so that they are prepared and do not disappear at the vital moment.

At buffets and informal weddings when there is no toastmaster, it is usual for the best man or woman to call the attention of the guests to the start of the cake-cutting ceremony. The bride and groom may then pose for photographs to be taken. The chief bridesmaid, if she is not making a speech, can then lead the call for a speech.

The traditional order of toasts has a certain logic. The first speech leads up to a toast to bride and groom, the most important people of the day. In effect, at a traditional first wedding they are the honoured guests of the hosts, her parents. But while as host her father can make a speech or toast to his new son-in-law, it would be a bit immodest for him to sing the praises of his own daughter, so often a friend of the family is chosen, particularly if the father is going to speak later. The honour of making the first speech may go to the best speaker or the best friend.

It falls upon the groom to reply to the first speech on behalf of himself and his bride. He will thank both his in-laws, especially if they've paid for or organized the wedding, and especially his mother-in-law. He should also thank anyone else who has helped, including the bridesmaids, and end with a toast to the bridesmaids and/or the Matron of Honour.

The bride may speak instead of or as well as her husband. If there are no bridesmaids the groom can make a toast to his bride, who can speak next in reply. The bride can propose a toast to the bridegroom if the first toast was to her alone, or to the bridesmaids or Matron of Honour. Alternatively she can propose a toast to the family of the bridegroom or, if they are not present, to the guests.

The best man or woman replies on behalf of the helpers (the bridesmaids). If there are no bridesmaids he does not have to speak, though he may wish to do so. The best man or the groom can end his speech with a toast to the hosts, and the bride's father or mother, or both, can reply. An optional toast to HM the Queen is made at most Jewish weddings in the UK.

Lastly the best man or the toastmaster reads the telegrams – in full if there are only a few, or reads the wittiest in full and then just gives the names of the senders of the others if there are many.

Variations to these customs can of course be made to suit differing circumstances and preferences, for instance at a second wedding or when no parents are present. If you are called upon to handle any surprise announcements, check that these are suitable and will not cause illwill. Announcements of engagements and forthcoming weddings of other guests could deflect attention from the bride. The announcement of the bride's sister's engagement would be acceptable, but only if the bride herself knows in advance and gladly agrees to the public announcement being made at her wedding.

Language Barriers

It can be a problem if, for example, the groom speaks no English: either he, or the bride and her family, may feel he ought to have the opportunity to speak at his own wedding, or that he has a duty to honour his hosts by thanking them publicly.

There are two solutions. Either he speaks in his own language and an interpreter delivers a translation; the translator can be the bride or another person. Or he can remain silent except for nodding, smiling and lifting his glass, allowing the bride to speak on their behalf, making due reference to him – my husband has asked me, etc.

The same system will be adopted if you have two receptions, one in each country. The speakers just have to do everything twice, taking note of which family is playing host.

Pre-wedding speeches

Various kinds of engagement and pre-wedding parties can be held and on such occasions, speeches are usually short, merely introducing the young couple, expressing pleasure at the engagement, and wishing them happiness. A parent of the bride or groom speaks or, if there are no parents present, another older relative playing host can make a speech. Here are some examples:

To the happy couple by the groom's (or the bride's) father / mother

I am delighted to welcome you to meet Steven's fiancée Annabelle and her family (or Annabelle's fiancé Steven and his family). They hope to marry next June, or sooner if they find a house. It is lovely to see you all, and so many friends from the old school and college and Steven's office (or from Annabelle's old school, etc.). Thank you so much for your good wishes. I hope everybody's got a glass of champagne – Have you? Good! Because I would like you to join me in wishing every happiness to Annabelle and Steven.

To Annabelle and Steven.

Reply and thanks to the host and guests by bride / groom and toast to the other family

I want to thank Mum and Dad for throwing this lovely party so that you could meet Annabelle and her family (or Steven and his family). Thank you all for coming this evening, and for bringing such generous presents. I'd like you to drink a toast to Annabelle's parents Betty and Jim (or to Steven's parents John and Clare).

To Betty and Jim (or John and Clare).

Thanks and toast to hosts by the other family

I'd like to thank Betty and Jim for organizing this wonderful party to give both of our families the ideal opportunity to get to know each other. And thank you everyone for welcoming us so wholeheartedly. Please join me in wishing good health to Betty and Jim.

To Betty and Jim.

Wedding speeches

The following sample speeches are to suit different situations and speakers. If you feel completely daunted at the thought of writing your own, choose the most appropriate speech and substitute your own details.

Toast to the bride and groom at an informal wedding reception

I would like to propose a toast to Annabelle and Steven, wishing them much joy and happiness for their future together. May all their troubles be little ones.

To Annabelle and Steven.

Toast to the bride and groom given by the bride's father

Reverend Brown, Ladies and Gentlemen, all my guests, I cannot tell you how pleased I am today to see my daughter Annabelle looking so radiantly happy, as she begins life as the wife of Steven. My wife and I do not feel that we are losing Annabelle, but entrusting her to Steven's good care. During the last few months as we have got to know him better, he has shown himself to be exactly the sort of person we had hoped Annabelle would marry – charming, sincere, reliable – with a clear idea of what he wants from life and how to achieve it. I know what his many friends and family, as well as those who have only recently met him, think that this must be one of those marriages that are made in heaven, and will want to join me in wishing Steven and Annabelle a long and happy married life together. So please stand and raise your glasses, and drink to the health and happiness of Annabelle and Steven. (Pause.)

To Annabelle and Steven.

Toast to the bride and groom given by an old friend or relative when the bride's father is present but does not make a speech

Annabelle's father, George, and her mother, Martha, have done me the honour of offering me the opportunity to make a speech on this wonderful occasion and propose a toast to Annabelle and Steven. When I asked why they chose me, George said, because you are the President of the Oxford Drama Club / my bank manager / my oldest friend / the boss / have known us for twenty-five years / you are the tallest / you have the loudest voice, and Martha said, because you have known Annabelle since she was fourteen / a baby / a child /

all her life / at school / at college / you tell the best jokes. I have seen Annabelle acting in school plays / at the drama club on many occasions but today she doesn't need to act, she has a starring role.

Seriously, over the years I have seen Annabelle develop many talents and accomplishments. She has won prizes for drama / music / essay-writing / cookery / coming top of her class in school / been awarded the first grade in music / drama, studied nursing / teaching / ballet / ice-skating / French and management / interviewing / accounting, learned how to drive / ski / sail / swim / dance / surf, followed her interests in travelling / bridge-playing / opera / the orchestra / film and reading science fiction / novels / biographies, as well as finding time to raise money for charity / do voluntary work with handicapped children / attend church functions regularly / design clothes / paint / draw and to help in her family's shop / business / company / restaurant. It was while she was at school / college / work, that she met Steven who was studying / working / travelling.

Though Steven had not yet qualified as a doctor / passed his A levels / opened his restaurant / learned to tell the difference between a gasket and a sprocket, it was obvious that they had much in common. (Or: At first it didn't look as if they had much in common.) But as they got to know each other Annabelle discovered that Steven liked the arts as much as the sciences / hiking as well as driving / driving cars as well as repairing them. And Steven learned that Annabelle could pilot a plane / ice a cake / run a playgroup / speak fluent French. And when Steven learned that Annabelle / Annabelle's father / mother / brother was an MP / barrister/had the best collection of Beatles records, that clinched it.

These young people have a bright future ahead of them, a wonderful career / job / home planned in London / New York / Sydney. And I am sure you will want to join me in wishing them every success and happiness in their new venture and marriage. Please raise your glasses and drink to the health and prosperity of Annabelle and Steven. (Pause.)

To Annabelle and Steven.

Toast to the bride and groom given by a friend or relative when the bride's father is recently deceased

It is my great pleasure to be here with you on this happy occasion and to help Annabelle and Steven celebrate their marriage. I have known Annabelle and her parents for many years, since I / we / they came to live in London / Glasgow / Cardiff.

Annabelle's late father, George, used to enjoy a game of football / a game of golf / fixing the car on Saturday afternoons, and we spent many happy hours together sailing / relaxing often accompanied by Steven. I remember George saying that Steven seemed to be a very pleasant / good-natured / hard-working / ambitious / talented young man. I know George and Steven got on well and George would have been delighted to have seen this happy day. Although we miss George's presence, and his unfailing good humour, we know that he was looking forward to this wedding and we have fulfilled his hopes and wishes, and in a sense he is with us today in our memories of him.

He would have been very satisfied to know what a comfort Steven has been to our family, how understanding, how supportive a friend in time of need, a valuable help to us in everything from fixing the car, taking over day-to-day decisions, to just being there when we wanted advice and assistance. The wedding was postponed, but Annabelle is a girl worth waiting for. Doesn't she look a picture today? George would have been proud of her, as I am sure Steven is. And it is with every confidence that I tell you I am sure that this young couple will have a very happy marriage, and I would ask you to join me in wishing them both a long, happy and prosperous future together. Please stand and lift your glasses. I propose a toast – to Annabelle and Steven. (Lift glass in air and wait for everybody to stand and raise glasses.)

To Annabelle and Steven.

Toast to the bride and groom given by an older man addressing a large, distinguished audience

Ladies and Gentlemen, it is always a pleasure to attend a wedding. They say that the world loves a lover and I think this is true. Marriage is the expression of love, and also the start of a lifelong adventure. Plato said, 'The beginning is the most important part of the work'. If that is the case, then Annabelle and Steven have been fortunate in enjoying the most wonderful beginning. They already have most of the good gifts one would wish upon a young couple. Annabelle is a beautiful bride, Steven is a handsome husband, and both come from secure family homes where their parents have set examples of what a good marriage should be.

A good marriage is not something you can create on your own without help from your partner. It is a joint venture. Marriage is like a journey in a boat. You cannot drill a hole in the boat and when water floods in say to your companion, 'It's nothing to do with you, the water is coming in on my side of the boat.' You must row in the same direction. In fact love has been defined as not looking at each other, but looking in the same direction.

If marriage is a boat, then many of us are in the same boat! Annabelle and Steven, you are embarking on a wonderful journey, and you have many friends who will support you, and help you, and wish you well. I would now like to ask everyone in this room to stand with me, and raise their glasses. (Pause briefly until noise of moving chairs ceases.) I propose a toast to the long life, health, wealth and happy marriage, of Annabelle and Steven.

To Annabelle and Steven!

Toast to the bride and groom given by the best man or woman

It gives me special pleasure to be present at the wedding of my good friends Annabelle and Steven, because I introduced them at the Dashing Disco / Royal Hotel / Country Club and because I have known both of them for many years at school / the tennis club. May their lives continue with equal joy and may they share many happy occasions and reunions such as this with our families and friends.

Here's to Annabelle and Steven.

Toast to the bride and groom given 'impromptu' by the best man at a very small wedding without bridesmaids

This is a lovely small, intimate gathering of friends which is just the way Annabelle and Steven wanted it to be. And we appreciate how honoured we are to be among the select few who they chose to share this very special occasion with them. Everyone here is a close friend or relative and we all have personal knowledge of Annabelle's unique qualities, her kindness, her gift for creating a happy atmosphere and her loyal friendship. And we are delighted that she is marrying Steven, who is so loved / admired by his family and close friends and is respected by all of us for his hard work / talents / skills / zest for life. He shares many of her good qualities and they both deserve all the good things in life. So let's wish them both a very happy married life together. Has everyone got a drink? Good.

To Annabelle and Steven.

Toast to the bride's parents given by the groom, replying to a toast to the bride and groom

Reverend Brown, Ladies and Gentlemen. (Pause.) Thank you very much, George, for those kind words. It goes almost without saying how pleased I am to be here today. In order not to dull your pleasure I intend to only speak for a few minutes in case we all get snowed in / melt away in the heat! We couldn't have wished for better weather – perfect sunshine, just the right start for a wedding day and honeymoon / the most beautiful, romantic white Christmas.

As you all know, Annabelle has been a much sought-after girl / woman, but I'm pleased to announce the winner of the competition, me. There are no runners up, or associated prizes.

My new mother-in-law, Martha, has worked long and hard for many months to prepare this wonderful occasion, all the little details such as these beautiful flower / cake decorations were planned by her, and my father-in-law has taken on his second mortgage without complaint, like the good-natured man he is. I am very pleased to be part of the same family and to know that my parents feel the same.

Speaking of whom, today represents a great occasion for both my parents, being the culmination of many years of planning of a different sort. They have prepared me well, supported me through university, taught me the difference between right and wrong, so that I know which I am enjoying at any given time!

Annabelle is beautiful, intelligent and hard-working. The list of her good qualities is extremely long. Unfortunately I cannot read her handwriting.

I would like to thank you all for your presence – in both senses of the word, but especially for the smiling faces I see in front of me. I am particularly pleased that Aunt Alice managed to make the long journey down to Surrey from Aberdeen for this occasion, and we are all delighted that Annabelle's sister, Sharon, flew all the way from Australia to join us and be such a charming bridesmaid. Of course she had a 'little help' – quite a big help, actually, from Tracey, who looked so sweet holding Annabelle's train.

My best man, Alan, has made everything go smoothly, and made his contribution to what has seemed the perfect day.

(Alternative ending: Finally, I must pay tribute to the brides-maids, Sharon, Natalie, Margaret and Sue, whose invaluable support has helped to make this day so successful.)

If there are no bridesmaids, the toast is to his parents-in-law as follows:

In conclusion, thank you, everybody, for listening, and I hope you are having a wonderful afternoon/evening and are all as happy as we are today. Would you kindly stand and raise your glasses, and drink a toast to the health of your hosts, two wonderful people, George and Martha. (Pause.)

To George and Martha!

Toast to the groom and both families given at an informal wedding by the bride

I'd like to propose a toast to the most wonderful man in the world, my new husband, Steven. I'd also like to thank his parents for what they have contributed over the years to make him the person he is, supporting him through college, and also for making me such a welcome member of their family. I must also thank my parents for everything they have done for me and especially this wonderful event, my wedding to Steven. May we all meet on many more happy occasions.

To Steven.

Toast to the bridesmaids given by the groom in reply to a toast to the bride and groom

My wife and I (pause for laughter), thank you for your kind words. It is wonderful to be surrounded by so many friends and good wishes. We have been overwhelmed by the kindness and help we have received, the generous gifts, and the people who have made extra contributions on this, our special day. I must mention the bridesmaids who have done so much to help my wife, and added glamour to the photographs which will remind us of this very happy occasion.

To the bridesmaids!

Toast to the groom's family given by the bride's father replying to the groom's toast to the bride's parents who are hosts (giving personal family marriage details)

Thank you, Steven. As you know, Annabelle is our only daughter, so this will be our only chance to stage such a lovely wedding. And we did not want to miss the opportunity of having such a wonderful day, complete with the white wedding car. When my grandparents' generation were marrying back in the 1920s not everyone had cars and the best man's responsibility was to organize transport for all the guests. After the ceremony the bridal couple rushed to the photographer's studio to have their portrait taken, before joining their guests who were waiting for the wedding meal. For each generation the circumstances are different. Now we can have a photographer visiting us to make a video, so that we can remember this magical day for the rest of our lives.

Martha and I married during the Sixties and many members of her family, living at the other end of the country, were unable to join us. Being a young apprentice, an overseas honeymoon was out of the question, so we went to a small cottage on the coast and it rained all the time we were there! Despite that, Martha and I had a wonderful wedding, and were very grateful to her parents for the wedding they gave us. But I think you will understand why we do not regret staging a grand wedding for Annabelle and Steven.

For us this has been our only chance to enjoy a wedding with all the luxuries and trimmings, and all our family around us. We want Annabelle and Steven to enjoy the things we never had, not to take them for granted, but to appreciate how lucky they are to be able to celebrate like this surrounded by their families and friends.

I know that Steven's parents understand how glad we are to do whatever we can for our daughter, and their son. We are very pleased to have Gregory and Gillian and their family here to celebrate with us. Their generous support and presence, joining in enthusiastically with everything we planned, has enabled us to truly enjoy this day. So please join me in drinking a toast to the health of my son-in-law's parents, Gregory and Gillian.

To Gregory and Gillian.

On a second or subsequent marriage it is frequently said that a wedding speech should make no reference to previous spouses, nor children of earlier marriages unless they are junior pages and need to be acknowledged and welcomed, or even the fact that either party has been married before. In theory you can use the usual wedding speeches, simply omitting any references to white weddings. However, rather than having the guests whispering conspiratorially amongst themselves the unmentionable secret that this is a second marriage, some speakers prefer a more direct and honest approach. This particularly applies where there is no question of a divorced previous spouse. It may be felt desirable to inform guests that one party was previously a devoted husband or wife, a widow or widower, who after years of loneliness should be congratulated on at last having found happiness again.

Toast to the bride and groom when a bride is marrying for the first time to a divorced man

Annabelle, for you this is a first marriage and a time of excitement and hope. For Steven it is a second marriage. He liked marriage so much that despite all the difficulties of his first attempt, when he met you he decided to try it again.

We hope that you will always enjoy life together, a very long and happy life together, and that you will always retain the enthusiasm of this new start, and remember the joy and delight of finding each other, which is so evident today. So we will all raise our glasses to you and toast your future.

To Annabelle and Steven.

Toast to the bride and groom when the groom is marrying for the first time to a divorced woman

Steven, for you this is a first marriage and a time of expectation and hope. For Annabelle it is a second marriage. You must be especially proud today, because she liked you so much that despite all the difficulties of her first marriage, when she met you she decided to try it again. What an honour!

We hope that both of you will always enjoy married life, and have a very long and happy life together. And that you will always retain the enthusiasm of this new start, and remember the joy and delight of finding each other, which is so evident today. So we will all raise our glasses to you and toast your future.

To Annabelle and Steven.

Toast to bride and groom, given by a friend on the occasion of a second or third marriage where both parties have been divorced or widowed at least once. Select part or all of the paragraphs as appropriate.

All marriages are special occasions but a second marriage is a doubly precious time because you do not take everything for granted. You realize how very lucky you are to be given another chance to be happy, and appreciate the blessing you have received in finding a soulmate and companion you can trust. It is a time of renewed hope.

I know that the two of you who are getting married today feel it is wonderful to be with so many good friends, and in particular one good friend, who understands your heartaches as well as your joys. That is so important.

It is a pleasure for you to experience an end to loneliness and sadness, and a joy for us to be witnesses and share this beginning with you. When you have experienced past disappointments, hardship and disillusionment, you know you have been up and down on life's waves. And when you are in the troughs of those waves, you sometimes wonder when you will ever come up again. Yet there is always a chance anew, an opportunity to feel love for someone, just like the first time. The past does not burden the present – but you learn by it, and do not repeat your mistakes. You have an opportunity through experience for knowing better than anyone else what is at stake and how much effort it takes, and what a loss it is if you don't do everything you can to make your partner contented. How fortunate you are to have found yet another chance at happiness together, with a better understanding than most people of what you should do to make a successful marriage and how much you will gain.

It is difficult late in life to put away the past, and start again, but you have all the means at your disposal to make a success of the venture. Everyone has the right to happiness, and should you have the chance to find happiness, whether you are someone young starting a new and joyful life again, or a grandmother, why not?

We are confident that you will now receive the joy you deserve, and we are really happy for you. I speak for everyone here when I say we wish you all the best, and hope that for you (pause) 'the best is yet to come'. So, Annabelle and Steven, we would like to drink a toast to your happy future together. (Raise glass.)

To Annabelle and Steven.

Wedding speeches to avoid

Sadly, you may well have been in the audience when one or more of these speeches has been delivered. However, it is best to remind you of them so that you can avoid following suit.

The over-apologetic speech

These usually start with 'I don't know why anyone picked me to give a speech. I've never given a speech in my life before. And I'm sure you don't want a long speech but I've tried to prepare something, and I hope it's all right. Anyway, all I can say is ... I did make some notes somewhere ... I think I put them in my pocket ... or maybe ...'. After dropped notes and all-round embarrassment, such a speech may conclude with 'Most of you don't know the groom, er, Alf, but I expect you'll want to wish him, and the bride of course, a happy, er, future.'

The negative and rather-too-revealing speech

Such as: 'I don't like speeches and I didn't want to give a speech but Martha insisted I should. I suppose there was nobody else. I'm not a good speaker so I'm not going to bore you by making a long speech.

Anne's a nice girl – I went out with her for a long time before she decided to marry Alfred, or he decided to marry her. So, I suppose it's what she wanted. Anyway, they know each other pretty well, having been living together for two years. They wouldn't have got married if she hadn't been pregnant, so the baby's done something good.' And may conclude with: 'Can I sit down now?'

The extremely brief reply

'Thank you.' This is not sufficient no matter how informal the wedding.

The depressing speech

If a close relative has recently died, avoid a speech like this:

'Relatives and friends, the one person missing here today is, of course, Anne's father, and no day can be really happy without him with us. Though I have tried to take his place, it is mere formality. No-one can take his place. Our happiness would have been complete if he had been here. Alas he is not ...'

This speech would probably reduce some of the guests, and almost certainly the bride and her mother, to tears.

The reluctant father-in-law's speech

Delivered thus:

'We're very pleased to see Anne getting married at last. When I first met Alfred I didn't like him very much, because of his hair and his clothes and the fact that he didn't have a steady job, but now I've got to know him he doesn't seem too bad. All these are things which can be changed. I'm sure Anne could change him if she wanted to, but she seems to like him the way he is ...'

At all costs, don't insult people.

The gushing speech

Commencing with:

'I am deeply honoured to be invited to this momentous and lavish occasion by my esteemed friends, Martha and George. It is a privilege to pay them this small token of respect. I am sure Martha will forgive me for saying that her very presence excites envy from others ...'

Everyone will cringe with embarrassment.

The long and pompous speech

This will continue at length along the lines of:

'Your Royal Highness, ladies and gentlemen, as a minister, judge and professor, I feel I am in a good position to speak about the history of marriage, its importance in society, and the duties of the married couple to each other and the wider community. First the history of marriage ...'

...until the speaker is probably stopped by a member of the bridal party.

Giving readings

If you are asked to read the lesson at a wedding, christening or funeral, treat the Bible as you would any other book. Make sense of what you read. Use imagination to colour and enhance mood, for it is rich in drama, poetry and pathos.

Although there are many serious and deep passages in the Bible, it should not be handled with kid gloves, or its words spoken with a 'special' voice. Delivered in soporific, chant-like tones, the message may become blurred and the congregation bored.

Modern versions of the Bible are now frequently used. However, the Authorized Version, with its beautiful use of language, is still read in some of the more traditional church services. Check with the bride and groom to find which version is more appropriate for their service. Use your modulatory skills you learnt in Chapter Three to bring passages to life. Remember to keep in touch with the sense of what is being said. Establish the mood and this will help you feel more involved with what is written.

Other celebrations

Anniversaries

Unless it is a very formal affair, an anniversary speech should appear impromptu but this does not mean it should be unprepared. Carry out similar research as described in the preparation of a wedding speech (see page 80). Any jokes or quotes should not appear forced.

Birthdays

Keep speeches happy and bright and perhaps restricted to a simple but sincere toast. If you know in advance that you will be giving a speech, use every opportunity to research the subject of your speech. As with weddings (see page 81), do not be tempted to insult your birthday guest and cause offence. There are many jokes and quotes referring to age to be found in Chapters Seven and Eight.

Christenings and naming ceremonies

Again, these should be happy and light and appear almost to be impromptu. A suitable toast for such an occasion would be 'May he/she enjoy long life, health, wealth and happiness.' Refer to Chapter Eight for suitable quotations about babies, children and parents. There are also some jokes to be found in Chapter Seven.

7

JOKES, COMIC STORIES AND ANECDOTES

On a happy occasion such as a wedding and at appropriate business and professional presentations, jokes and comic stories are welcome and can make a particularly good ending for a speech. If you cannot tell long jokes without getting lost, stick to one-liners. Try out each of your jokes on someone who will not be at the occasion to see if it sounds funny the way you tell it.

Apart from books of quotations and joke books, turn for advice to witty friends for other jokes to add to your repertoire. When constructing a funny story remember that one of the elements of humour in the punchline is surprise, going suddenly from the sublime to the ridiculous, from exhilaration to despair, from discovery of a tragedy to self-centred concern about some minor problem.

Avoiding unsuitable subject matter

The Victorians said that at the dinner table you should not discuss sex, politics or religion. Similarly the same will apply to any public speaking. Statements about religion or politics might result in a quarrel or give offence by causing people with opposing views to disagree, insult each other, or try to convert each other. Sexual references might give offence, as can double entendres. As a general rule you should avoid unintentionally offending but instead flatter or compliment them.

If your audience is Irish, even if you are Irish, you do not want a joke which makes Irish people appear stupid, but clever instead. The same applies to any other national or religious group. Remember that unless you have inspected the guest list or names of business delegates, you can never be sure of who is in the audience.

A short compendium of joke themes

The following are listed under theme and subject matter and can be adapted, as necessary, for different occasions.

Actors

I come not to bury Caesar but to praise (bridegroom's name). When an accomplished actor like (bridegroom's name) realizes he is going to have a speaking part in the wedding ceremony he jumps at the opportunity. Alas, being the best man at an actor's wedding is like trying to direct an actor who wants to direct. At the wedding rehearsal we got the video camera out and (bridegroom's name) said, 'To do or not to do ...' Then he asked who was the understudy.

As an actor myself, I wanted a part, too, but there isn't a speaking part for the best man at a wedding ceremony. So (bridegroom's name) very kindly invited me to give a speech. I was a trifle nervous when I remembered all the films I'd seen about weddings. There's *Jane Eyre* where the wedding is interrupted by someone who says the groom is already married. When we did the rehearsal again and Steven got it right I asked myself, has he played this scene before? Worse still, on the day, how could I be sure, with so many actors around, that the bridesmaids wouldn't turn out to be actors in drag? You can imagine my relief now that it's all over, and that it has turned out to be such a beautiful, conventional, dream wedding. They played their parts perfectly.

Argument

If you want the last word in an argument say, 'I expect you are right.'

Birthdays

The only sure way to remember your spouse's birthday is to forget it once.

Youth is a wonderful thing. It's such a pity it's wasted on the young.

Middle age is when someone's hair starts turning from grey to black.

He's / she's so old every time he / she goes into an antique shop someone tries to buy her.

There were so many candles on the birthday cake it melted.

When he lit all the candles on his birthday cake, three people collapsed from the heat.

I never forget (name)'s birthday. It's the day after they remind me of it.

Builders / decorators

It is harder to build than to destroy.

Children

As my wife tucks our youngster into bed each night she always says, 'Darling, if there is anything you want during the night, just call Mummy – and I'll send Daddy in.'

There is only one way I can make my children notice that I've got home from the office – I walk in front of the television set.

A three-year-old child gets more fun from the cardboard box than from the expensive present it contained.

Children are the ups and downs of life. They get you down all day and keep you up all night.

Cigarettes

I decided to give up cigarettes in two stages. First I'm going to give up smoking my cigarettes ... and then I'll give up smoking other people's.

Cinema / theatre / wedding ushers / usherettes

A woman in the audience / church left in the middle of the performance / wedding and as she left she trod on the foot of the man at the end of the row. When she returned she said, 'Did I tread on your foot on the way out?'

'Yes,' he replied.

'Good!' she said, 'Then this is my row.'

Committees

A camel is a horse which got designed by a committee.

Computer operators

President Kennedy said to an astronaut, 'Man is still the most extraordinary computer of all.'

To err is human. To really foul things up requires a computer.

Always check computerized bills. When we had just married our only gas consumption was the cooker, but we had a bill which would have enabled us to have cooked meals for the whole of Harrow.

Craftsperson

I asked (bride's / groom's name) what he / she did and he / she said 'I'm a craftsperson.'

   'Ah,' I said, 'Crafty, eh?'

Cricket

I'm often asked to explain the rules of cricket. A cricket game lasts up to five days. There are eleven players in each team. We do not follow the decimal system. That's 'not cricket'. We do not follow the British system of counting in dozens. That is not cricket. We count in elevenses. That is cricket. Three important words are 'in' and 'out' and 'over'. In cricket there is a wicket. One man strands near the wicket and bats and another bowls. The batsman is in. If he knocks down the wicket with his own leg, he is out. If he hits the ball he runs. There's another batsman who runs too, in the opposite direction. Every six balls they change the bowler. That's called an over. But the game isn't over. Not until they're all out. That's not the end of the game either, just the end of the innings. Now you know all the ins and outs of crickets. Simple, isn't it!

Dancing

We had to ask the bridesmaids not to pirouette in the aisle.

The bride was going to get married in a tutu but we persuaded her against it.

Dentists / dental technicians

What makes you nervous about them is that when you go to dinner with them, they pump up the chair.

Doctors / nurses / medical

In the dress rehearsal when she held out her finger for the ring he took her pulse. In the dress rehearsal when he held out the ring to her she took his pulse.

We have three empty seats today. One of these was for a doctor who has gone to the Middlesex Hospital. The other seats were for a couple who didn't know their way here and decided to follow his / her car. We just had a call from them. They're at the Middlesex Hospital and want to know the way back.

Most doctors have three things on their mind: ill, pill and bill. But he's / she's such a successful doctor he / she can afford to tell the patients when there's nothing wrong with them.

Good doctors aim to add life to your years, not just years to your life.

Drinking a toast

A glass of wine / whisky / champagne is said to cure all sorts of ills such as the common cold. All you need is a candle and a glass of wine / whisky / champagne. Light the candle, drink the first glass and wait five minutes. Drink another glass and wait, still watching the candle. Keep drinking until you see three candles, then snuff out the middle one and go to sleep.

Drivers (of buses, taxis, cars, lorries)

The French chauffeurs / Israeli motorists / Glasgow / Dublin drivers / East End taxi drivers / bus drivers, like (name) and his Dad are skilful, safe drivers. I was in a car / taxi / bus once which shot through a red light. At the next crossing it shot through another red light. The third light was green and it skidded to a halt. 'Why did you do that?' I asked.

He (name) said, 'You can't be too careful. There could have been another car/coach/taxi coming the other way!'

Economy

Charles Dickens had some advice on budgeting. The character Mr Micawber was based on Dickens's father and according to Dickens, Mr Micawber said, 'Annual income twenty pounds, annual expenditure nineteen and sixpence, result happiness. Annual income twenty pounds, annual expenditure twenty pounds and sixpence, result misery.' (Pause.) Mr Micawber's problem was he didn't have an account at (name subject of story's bank / business).

Jane Austen said, 'It is a truth universally acknowledged, that a single man in possession of a good fortune must be in want of a wife.' However, she must also have been thinking of (bride's name) when she added, 'She was of course only too good for him: but as nobody minds what is too good for them, he was very steadily earnest in pursuit of the blessing.'

Education

Something which enables you to pass out insults and call it repartee.

What is left after you have forgotten everything you have been taught.

Egotist

One of the nicest things about an egotist is that he never talks about other people.

I wouldn't say he's conceited – but with the whole world to fall in love with, he chose himself.

Estate agents

Estate agents have two types of house: the ones you don't want and the ones you can't afford.

Farmers and footballers

Football coach Bear Bryant is also a farmhand and in the old days farmhands used to guide a team of animals in front of the plough, encouraging them and making sure they all pulled together. But he also coaches a football team and his secret for teamwork is this. What he says is that if anything goes badly, he tells the team, 'I did it.' If anything goes reasonably well, he says, 'We did it!' But when everything goes really well, he says to them, 'You did it!' Marriage / work is not a game: it is a team.

Food industry

It is said that Colman's Mustard made their money from the amount of mustard left on the plate.

A customer asked (name) if the fruit salad was fresh. 'Yes,' he / she said, 'fresh last week!'

Gardeners / grocers / greengrocers

George has the best fruit / fruit trees. One day a little boy was standing looking at his apples / apple trees. George said, 'Were you trying to take an apple?'

The little boy answered, 'No. I was trying not to take an apple.'

Gloves

Something that keeps one hand warm while you look for its mate.

Golfers

Golf has been defined as a good walk spoilt.

All is fair in love and golf.

One thing you should remember: when he / she said, 'I just made a hole in one,' don't say, 'I didn't see you. Do it again.'

Hangover

Today is one of those days because last night was one of those nights.

Jogging

Jogging can really increase your body awareness. I've now got aching muscles in places where I never knew I had muscles.

Jogging is great for losing weight. I now buy my jogging shorts in three sizes – May, July and September.

The trouble with jogging is that by the time you realize you are not fit enough to do it, you've got a long walk home.

Journalists / printers / newsagents

A journalist is someone who hears shouts from a river, rushes up and asks, 'Are you all right?' When the man shouts back, 'I'm drowning,' the journalist replies, 'You're out of luck. You've missed the evening edition, but we can give you a paragraph in the morning edition.'

A journalist tries to get into places other people are trying to get out of.

Some journalists work for the paper read by the people who run the country (*The Times*). Some journalists work for the paper read by the people who think they run the country (*Daily Telegraph*). Some journalists work for the paper read by the spouses of people who run the country (*Daily Mail, Daily Express*). Some journalists work for the paper read by the people who would like to run the country but know they aren't likely to. And some journalists work for the paper whose readers don't care who runs the country as long as the girl on page three is well endowed.

(Adapt this as appropriate e.g. 'But [name] works for the paper read by the people who want to buy a Ford Granada for fourpence.)

Lawyers / judges / solicitors

A jury consists of twelve persons chosen to decide who has the better lawyer. (Robert Frost)

Luck

I'm so unlucky that if ever my ship comes in there will probably be a dock strike on.

Managers

The secret of good management is, never put off until tomorrow what you can get someone else to do today, especially if you want it done yesterday.

Marriage

They got married ... and lived nappily ever after.

Marriage is like a three-ring circus. First there's the engagement ring, next the wedding ring and then the suffer-ring.

Money

Always borrow money from a pessimist. He won't expect to get it back.

Narrow-mindedness

He is so narrow-minded he can look through a keyhole with both eyes at the same time.

Philosophy

A philosopher is a man who, when you ask how his wife is, replies, 'In relation to whom?'

Politics

Politics is not a bad profession. If you succeed there are many rewards. If you disgrace yourself you can always write a book. (Ronald Reagan)

Post Office workers

They deliver letters everywhere, even the cemetery – Dead Letters.

Psychiatrists and psychologists

I am often asked the difference between a psychologist and a psychiatrist. I say that a psychologist deals with the things normal people say and do, while a psychiatrist deals with the things dotty people say and do. When two psychologists are in a lift and a man gets into the lift and says hello, one psychologist turns to another and asks, 'What do you think he meant by that?'

Public speakers

Most speakers have four speeches: what they have prepared, what they actually say, what they wish they had said, and what they are quoted as saying.

Advice to speakers: If you don't strike oil in the first two minutes you'd better stop boring.

Rarity

There is nothing so rare as a juggernaut driver with an inferiority complex.

Self-defence

The first lesson in the art of self-defence is to keep your glasses on.

Speed

Every time I start thinking that the world is moving too fast, I go to the Post Office.

Sport

Wellington said that the Battle of Waterloo was won on the playing fields of Eton.

Did you hear about the idiot who was given a pair of water skis for his birthday? He's spent the last six months looking for a lake with a slope.

Statisticians

Everybody asks me what a statistician does. This story will explain it. A treasury statistician came down the steps of the ministry and met a beggar who held out his hand and said, 'Spare some change, mister? I haven't eaten for a week!

The statistician replied, 'Really? And how does that compare with the same period last year?'

Surprise

I love surprises as long as I'm ready for them.

Teachers

One of the most difficult tasks of a teacher is to tell a father that his son can't cope with the new maths. But you can soften the blow by telling his Dad that none of the other dads can do it either.

Telephone

Have you ever noticed that wrong numbers are never busy?

Television

On television, detective series end at just the right moment, after the criminal has been caught and before the courts turn him loose.

Tennis players

(Bride) and (groom) are both tennis players – the perfect match.

Temper

I never lose my temper but, I must admit, I do mislay it occasionally.

Vets/pet lovers

Vets have very strange conversations on the phone. Sometimes they are on the phone at someone else's house and a call is referred from a dog-owner and a relative hears them saying, 'And how is his third leg?'

Wedding customs

The French have some amusing wedding customs. When the dance music starts they play games. The first time the music stops every man gives his right shoe to his partner. Then he turns and dances with the woman behind. Next time the music stops he gives away his left shoe and again takes the partner behind. Then the woman gives away her right shoe, then her left shoe, then the man removes his jacket, then his tie. After the music stops for the last time the first man to return the ladies' shoes and collect up all his clothing is allowed to kiss every woman in the room!

Wills

My aunt had a cat and a parrot. When she died she left all of her estate to the cat. Now the parrot is contesting the will.

Work

Some people like to rest. I like work. I can enjoy watching it for hours. Others are workaholics who cannot stop working. Pius XII said to doctors who told him to cut down on his work schedule, 'I shall be able to rest one minute after I die.'

Of every 100 people in this country 55 per cent are of working age. At any one time 15 per cent are unemployed, that leaves 40 per cent. Of these, 5 per cent are sick, leaving 35 per cent. Of these, 5 per cent are on strike, leaving 30 per cent. At this time of year 20 per cent are on holiday, leaving 10 per cent. And of these, 8 per cent are looking after children or relatives. That leaves you and me. So all the work will have to be done by (name the subject/s of the story).

It's finally happened – the deductions have exceeded my salary. Last month the company didn't send me a cheque; they sent me a bill.

Salaries vary according to viewpoint. The factor that determines whether a wage is small or large is whether you are the employed or the employee.

There ought to be a better way to start the day than by getting up in the morning.

Office Rules:

1 The managing director is always right.

2 If the managing director is wrong Rule One applies.

I don't mind going to work. I don't mind coming home. It's the bit in the middle I don't like.

Have you seen the latest, simplified tax forms? All they ask is: What do you make? What do you spend? What have you got left? Send it to us!

We are sorry you are leaving. You are going to be hard to replace ... at the wage we've been paying you.

I hold a very responsible job. Anything goes wrong, I'm responsible.

Our computer doesn't actually do anything. We just blame it for everything.

Writers

When Agatha Christie was asked where she got her plots she replied, 'Harrods'.

8

QUOTATIONS AND PROVERBS

Add spice to your speeches and toasts by inserting an amusing, interesting or relevant quotation or proverb. This chapter includes a selection of quotations for the most common subjects you are likely to want to cover: love, marriage, weddings, family, work and hobbies, and so on. Libraries and bookshops will, of course, stock treasuries of quotations. Consider using quotes from well-known humorous writers including James Thurber, Charles Dickens, Mark Twain, Jane Austen, Oscar Wilde, George Bernard Shaw and William Shakespeare.

Songwriters are another good source of quotable lines. You can track down the words of songwriters from books of librettos or some CD sleeves. Good songwriters to quote include W. S. Gilbert, Sammy Cahn and Noël Coward. Alternatively, refer to a good dictionary of popular music.

American quotations can be found among the saying of every president from Washington, Jefferson, Lincoln, Roosevelt and Kennedy to Reagan, Bush and Clinton. Politics, business, morality, and determination to win against the odds are popular subjects. *The Oxford Companion to American Literature* will help to locate American novels, plays and other books.

Unless you are a great actor or orator, avoid any verse over four lines long. Five-line limericks, however, add humour, but be sure they are in good taste. Seek them out in a good poetry anthology.

Adapting quotations

The more you can relate your quotations to your audience and your subject matter, the more interested they will be. If the only quotation you can find is not very relevant or complimentary, adapt it. For example, at the wedding of a soldier you could start, 'According to the British Grenadiers, "Some talk of Alexander, and some of Hercules, and others of Lysander and such great names as these." But I would rather talk about Captain (groom's name).'

A selection of quotations and proverbs

To make the quotations more suitable for delivery in speech, some have been updated to include a more colloquial approach.

Acting and law

The law and the stage – both are a form of exhibition. (Orson Welles)

Actors

Actors are never out of work. They are always resting.

When an actor has money he doesn't send letters; he sends telegrams. (Anton Chekhov)

Advertising

A picture is worth a thousand words.

Half the money spent on advertising is wasted, but we don't know which half.

Advice

In giving advice I advise you, be short. (Horace)

When angry, count to a hundred. (Mark Twain)

Tact is the art of making a point without making an enemy. The most difficult thing in the world is to know how to do a thing and to watch someone else doing it wrong and keep quiet.

Live within your means, even if you have to borrow money to do it.

God helps them that help themselves. (Benjamin Franklin)

Look before you leap,
For as you sow, you're likely to reap. (Samuel Butler)

To err is human: to forgive, divine.

Education forms the common mind:
Just as the twig is bent, the tree's inclined. (Alexander Pope)

If you can fill the unforgiving minute
With sixty seconds' worth of distance run
Yours is the earth and everything that's in it,
And – which is more – you'll be a man, my son. (Rudyard Kipling)

Be thou familiar, but by no means vulgar ...
costly thy habit as thy purse can buy.
But not expressed in fancy; rich, not gaudy,
For the apparel oft proclaims the man.
Neither a borrower or a lender be;
For oft the loan loses both itself and friend,
And borrowing dulls the edge of husbandry
This above all: to thine own self be true,
And it must follow, as the night the day,
Thou canst not then be false to any man.
Farewell; my blessing season this in thee. (William Shakespeare, Polonius' speech to Laertes in *Hamlet*)

To be prepared is half the victory. (Miguel de Cervantes)

A place for everything and everything in its place. (Samuel Smiles)

A knife of the keenest steel requires the whetstone, and the wisest man needs advice. (Zoroaster)

Don't put it down, put it away.

Age

You know you've reached middle age when your weight-lifting consists merely of standing up. (Bob Hope)

One has to be seventy before one is full of courage. The young are always half-hearted. (D. H. Lawrence)

Age brings wisdom. American millionaire, Bernard Baruch, said that, 'an elder statesman is somebody old enough to know his mind – and keep quiet about it'. (Joe E. Lewis)

You're only young once, and if you work it right, once is enough. (Joe E. Lewis)

Wrinkles should merely indicate where smiles have been. (Mark Twain)

Grow old along with me!
The best is yet to be. (Robert Browning)

The four stages of man are infancy, childhood, adolescence and obsolescence. (Art Linklater, *A Child's Garden of Misinformation*)

Time still, as he flies, adds increase to her truth,
And gives to her mind what he steals from her youth. (Edward Moore)

Ambition

He who aims at the moon may hit the top of a tree; he who aims at the top of a tree is unlikely to get off the ground.

I don't want to achieve immortality through my work. I want to achieve immortality by not dying. (Woody Allen)

Ambition can creep as well as soar. (Edmund Burke)

By the time a person gets to greener pastures, he can't climb the fence. (Frank Dickson)

Hitch your wagon to a star. (Ralph Waldo Emerson)

The idea that to make a man work you've got to hold gold in front of his eyes is a growth, not an axiom. We've done that for so long that we've forgotten there's any other way. (F. Scott Fitzgerald, *This Side of Paradise*)

Spoon feeding, in the long run, teaches nothing but the shape of the spoon. (E. M. Forster)

When written in Chinese the word crisis is composed of two characters. One represents danger and the other represents opportunity. (John F. Kennedy)

Only a mediocre person is always at his best. (W. Somerset Maugham)

If you don't want to work, you have to work to earn enough money so that you won't have to work. (Ogden Nash)

An aim in life is the only fortune worth finding. (Robert Louis Stevenson)

No-one knows what he can do till he tries. (Publius Syrus)

Anger

Every minute you spend being angry with your partner is a waste of sixty seconds in which you could be enjoying yourselves.

The second blow makes the fray. (Francis Bacon)

If you argue and rankle and contradict, you may achieve a victory sometimes; but it will be an empty victory because you will never get your opponent's goodwill. (Benjamin Franklin)

Appearance

If you actually look like your passport photo, you aren't well enough to travel.

Confidence is simply that quiet, assured feeling you have just before you fall flat on your face. (Dr L. Binder)

Babies

A baby is an alimentary canal with a loud voice at one end and no responsibility at the other. (E. Adamson)

There are two things in this life for which we are never fully prepared. Twins. (John Billings)

When baby's cries grew harder to bear,
I popped him in the Frigidaire.
I never would have done so if
I'd known he'd be frozen stiff.
My wife said 'George, I'm so unhappy,
Our darling's now completely frappé.' (Harry Graham, *More Ruthless Rhymes*)

A bit of talcum,
Is always walcum. (Ogden Nash, *Reflections of Babies*)

Bachelors

He could have made many women happy by remaining a bachelor. He could also have made one woman happy by remaining a bachelor.

Advice to those about to marry. Don't. (*Punch*, 1845)

When a lady's in the case,
You know, all other things give place. (John Gay)

A man is so in the way in the house. (Mrs Gaskell)

His designs were strictly honourable, as the phrase is; that is, to rob a lady of her fortune by way of marriage. (Henry Fielding)

Beauty

Beauty is in the eye of the beholder.

Blame

To err is human; to blame it on someone else is more so.

Blessings, thanks, prayers and hopes

The Lord is my shepherd; I shall not want ...
Surely goodness and mercy shall follow me all the days of my life. (*Psalm 23*. A Psalm of David)

Business

The business of America is business. (President Calvin Coolidge)

There's no business like show business. (Song lyric)

Caution

Guard against the fellow who slaps you on the back. It could be to help you swallow something.

He that is over-cautious will accomplish little. (Friedrich Schiller)

Cheerfulness

Cheerfulness in doing renders a deed more acceptable. (Fuller)

Children

The little one lies in its cradle
The little one sits in its chair
And the light of heaven above
Transfigures its golden hair. (Adapted from *The Changeling* by James Russell Lowell)

Children are your heritage, like arrows in the hand of the mighty man. Happy is the man who has his quiver full of them. (Adapted from *Psalm 127*)

May your wife be like a fruitful vine growing by the side of your house, and your children like olive plants round about your table. (Adapted from *Psalm 128*)

Anybody who hates children and dogs can't be all bad. (W. C. Fields)

One of the most obvious facts about grown-ups to a child is that they have forgotten what it is like to be a child. (Randall Jarrell, *Third Book of Criticism*)

There is only one beautiful child in the world, and every mother has it. (Stephen Leacock)

My mother loved children – she would have given anything if I had been one. (Groucho Marx)

The more people have studied different methods of bringing up children the more they have come to the conclusion that what good mothers and fathers instinctively feel like doing for their babies is best after all. (Dr Benjamin Spock, *The Commonsense Book of Baby and Child Care*)

Monday's child is fair of face,
Tuesday's child is full of grace;
Wednesday's child is full of woe,
Thursday's child has far to go;
Friday's child is loving and giving,
Saturday's child works hard for its living;
and the child that's born on the Sabbath day,
is fair and wise and good and gay.

I have found the best way to give advice to your children is to find out what they want and then advise them to do it. (Harry S. Truman)

Youngsters today have so many luxuries that the best way to punish your child is to send him to your room instead of his. (Earl Wilson)

Committees

A committee is an animal with four back legs. (John Le Carré, *Tinker, Tailor, Soldier, Spy*)

A committee is a group of the unwilling, picked from the unfit, to do the unnecessary. (Richard Harkness)

Divorce

We pondered whether to take a holiday or get a divorce, and we decided that a trip to Bermuda is over in two weeks, but a divorce is something you always have. (Woody Allen)

Doubts

Give me the benefit of your convictions, if you have any; but keep your doubts to yourself, for I have enough of my own. (Johann von Goethe)

Drinking, toasts and drunkenness

A toast to sweethearts. May all sweethearts become married couples and may all married couples remain sweethearts.

Here's to the bride and groom. May their happiness last forever and may we be fortunate enough to continue being part of it.

We'll drink a cup of kindness yet, for the sake of old lang syne. (Adapted from Robert Burns)

The best cure for drunkenness is while sober to see a drunken man. (Chinese proverb)

Drink to me only with thine eyes,
And I will pledge with mine;

Or leave a kiss within the cup,
And I'll not look for wine. (Ben Jonson)

Champagne and orange juice is definitely a great drink. The orange improves the champagne. The champagne improves the orange. (Prince Philip)

Enthusiasm

Nothing great was ever achieved without enthusiasm. (Ralph Waldo Emerson)

Expectation

Blessed is he who expects nothing, for he shall never be disappointed. (Alexander Pope)

Expertise

Make three correct guesses consecutively and everyone will regard you as an expert.

An expert is one who knows more and more about less and less. (Nicholas Murray Butler)

Sometimes men come by the name of genius in the same way an insect comes by the name of centipede – not because it has a hundred feet, but because most people can't count above fourteen. (George Lichtenberg)

Families

Important families are like potatoes. The best parts are underground. (Francis Bacon)

The apple does not fall far from the tree. (Proverb)

Everyone is the son of his own works. (Miguel de Cervantes, *Don Quixote*)

The child is father of the man. (William Wordsworth)

Winston Churchill said, a family starts 'with a young man falling in love with a girl. No superior alternative has been found.'

A man must first govern himself ere he is fit to govern a family. (Sir Walter Raleigh)

Father

A father of the fatherless is God. (*Psalm 68*)

Honour thy father and thy mother. (Old Testament)

Fear

He that is afraid to shake the dice will never throw a six. (Chinese proverb)

Fools

Only a fool tests the depth of the water with both feet. (African proverb)

Everyone is a damn fool for at least five minutes every day. Wisdom is not exceeding the limit. (Elbert Hubbard)

Forgiveness

The more a man knows the more he forgives. (Catherine the Great)

Forgiveness needs to be accepted, as well as offered, before it is complete. (C. S. Lewis)

Friendship

No man is useless while he has a friend. (Robert Louis Stevenson)

One man in a thousand, Solomon says,
Will stick more close than a brother.
But the thousandth Man will stand by your side
To the gallows-foot – and after! (Rudyard Kipling)

A faithful friend is the medicine for life. (Ecclesiasticus)

Happiness consists not in the multitude of friends but in their worth and choice. (Ben Jonson)

(The only way) to have a friend is to be one. (Ralph Waldo Emerson)

Gardens

God the first garden made. (Abraham Cowley)

One is nearer God's heart in the garden
Than anywhere else on earth. (Dorothy Gurney)

Our England is a garden, and such gardens are not made
By singing: – 'Oh, how beautiful!' and sitting in the shade.
(Rudyard Kipling)

Grandparents and grandchildren

I don't know who my grandfather was. I am much more concerned to know what his grandson will be. (Abraham Lincoln)

Greatness

A great man shows his greatness by the way he treats little men.
(Thomas Carlyle)

There is a great man who makes every man feel small. But the real great man is the man who makes every man feel great. (Charles Dickens)

Greed

There is a sufficiency in the world for man's need but not for man's greed. (Mahatma Gandhi)

Guests

Too late I stayed, – forgive the crime;
Unheeded flew the hours.
How noiseless falls the foot of time,
That only treads on flowers! (Hon. William Robert Spencer)

Laugh and be merry together, like brothers akin,
Guesting awhile in the room of a beautiful inn.
Glad till the dancing stops, and the lilt of the music ends.
Laugh till the game is played; and be you merry my friends. (John Masefield, *Laugh and be Merry*)

Handwriting

Like the lesser rivers on maps. (Dorothy Parker)

Happiness

Not in doing what you like best, in liking what you do is the secret of happiness. (J. M. Barrie)

The greatest happiness of the greatest number. (Jeremy Bentham)

Happy is the man who can make a living by his hobby. (George Bernard Shaw)

Haste

Haste is the mother of imperfection. (Brazilian proverb)

Health and wealth

If you enjoy good health, you are rich.

Early to bed and early to rise makes a man healthy, wealthy and wise.

I wish you health; I wish you wealth; I wish you gold in store; I wish you heaven when you die; what could I wish you more?

Home and away

East, west, home is best.

There is no place like home after the other places close.

If solid happiness we prize,
Within our breast this jewel lies;

And they are fools who roam;
The world has nothing to bestow;
From our own selves our joys must flow,
And that dear place – our home. (Nathaniel Cotton)

Wherever I roam, whatever realms I see,
My heart untravelled fondly turns to thee. (Oliver Goldsmith)

't is distance lends enchantment to the view,
And robes the mountain in its azure hue. (Thomas Campbell)

Honesty

Honest is the cat when the milk's away. (Cheales)

The best measurement of a man's honesty isn't his income tax return. It's the zero adjustment on his bathroom scales. (Arthur C. Clarke)

House

I often wish that I had clear,
For life, six hundred pounds a year,
A handsome house to lodge a friend,
A river at my garden's end. (Jonathan Swift)

Humour

Humour cannot be learnt. Besides wit and keenness of mind, it presupposes a large measure of goodness of heart, of patience, of tolerance and of human kindness. (Curt Goetz)

Everything is funny as long as it is happening to somebody else. (Will Rogers)

Husbands

American women expect to find in their husbands a perfection that English women only hope to find in their butlers.

Being a husband is a whole-time job. (Arnold Bennett)

Marrying a man is like buying something you've been admiring in a shop window. You may love it when you get home, but it doesn't always go with everything else in the house. (Jean Kerr, *The Snake has all the Lines*)

Husbands love your wives and do not be bitter against them. (New Testament, *Colossians*)

Kindness

The whole worth of a kind deed lies in the love that inspires it. (The Talmud)

One of the most difficult things to give away is kindness – it is usually returned.

Law

Good laws make it easier to do right and harder to do wrong. (William Gladstone)

I was never ruined but twice, once when I lost a lawsuit and once when I was one. (Voltaire)

Laziness

Anybody who isn't pulling his weight is probably pushing his luck.

He who is carried on another's back does not appreciate how far off the town is. (African proverb)

Leadership

If anyone has a new idea in this country, there are twice as many people who advocate putting a man with a flag in front of it. (Prince Philip)

If a man does only what is required of him, he is a slave. The moment he does more, he is a free man. (A. W. Robertson)

Some are born great, some achieve greatness, and some have greatness thrust upon them. (William Shakespeare, *Twelfth Night)*

You must learn to obey before you command. (Solon)

There are no gains without pains. (Adlai Stevenson)

A new broom sweeps clean, but the old one finds the corners. (H. W. Thompson)

The person who knows how will always have a job. But the person who knows why will be boss. (Carl Wood)

Life

Life is what happens to you while you're making other plans. (Robert Balzer)

Life is like a sewer. What you get out of it depends on what you put in to it. (Tom Lehrer, *We Will All Go Together When We Go)*

We may live without poetry, music and art;
We may live without conscience and live without books;
But civilised man cannot live without cooks. (Lord Lytton)

The art of public life consists to a great extent of knowing exactly where to stop and going a bit further. (H. H. Munro)

The ideal man is healthy and fit and has a well-trained mind. The bookworm and the gladiator are only half-trained men, leading only half a life. (Prince Philip)

Our life is frittered away by detail ... simplify, simplify. (Henry David Thoreau)

Besides the noble art of getting things done, there is the noble art of leaving things undone. The wisdom of life consists in the elimination of non-essentials. (Lin Yutang)

If men could regard the events of their own lives with more open minds they would frequently discover that they did not really desire the things they failed to obtain. (André Maurois, *The Art of Living)*

Do all the good you can,
By all the means you can,
In all the ways you can,
In all the places you can,
At all the times you can,
To all the people you can,
As long as ever you can. (John Wesley)

Losing

The only time losing is more fun than winning is when you're fighting temptation. (Tom Wilson)

Love

And to his eye
There was but one beloved face on earth
And that was shining on him. (Lord Byron)

Love and marriage go together like a horse and carriage. (Sammy Cahn, song lyric)

None but the brave deserve the fair. (John Dryden)

When one loves somebody everything is clear – where to go, what to do – it all takes care of itself and one doesn't have to ask anybody about anything. (Maxim Gorky, *The Zykovs*)

The meeting of two personalities is like the contact of two chemical substances; if there is any reaction, both are transformed. (Carl Jung)

A thing of beauty is a joy forever. (John Keats)

Whoever loved that love not at first sight? (Christopher Marlowe)

Love does not consist in gazing at each other, but in looking outward in the same direction. (Antoine de Saint-Exupéry)

The course of true love never did run smooth. (William Shakespeare, *A Midsummer Night's Dream*)

Love is as strong as death. (*The Song of Solomon* 8:6)

In the spring a young man's fancy lightly turns to thoughts of love. (Alfred, Lord Tennyson, *Locksley Hall*)

The first duty of love is to listen. (Paul Tillich)

Love conquers all. (Virgil)

Whatever you do ... love those who love you. (Voltaire)

Luck

Of course I believe in luck. How else can you explain the success of the people you detest? (Jean Cocteau)

Marriage

Happiness in marriage is entirely a matter of chance. (Jane Austen)

The critical period in matrimony is breakfast time. (A. P. Herbert)

Marriage has many pains, but celibacy has no pleasures. (Dr Samuel Johnson)

The most difficult year of marriage is the one you're in. (Franklin P. Jones)

When you are bored with yourself, marry and be bored with someone else. (David Pryce-Jones, *Owls and Satyrs*)

Marriage is like a cage; one sees the birds outside desperate to get in; and those inside desperate to get out. (Michel de Montaigne)

The great secret of a successful marriage is to treat all disasters as incidents and none of the incidents as disasters. (Harold Nicolson)

I've been married so many times my certificate now reads: 'To whom it may concern.' (Mickey Rooney)

Marriage is a bargain and somebody has to get the worst of a bargain. (Helen Rowland)

A successful marriage requires falling in love many times – with the same person.

Here's to marriage, that happy estate that resembles a pair of scissors: 'So joined that they cannot be separated, often moving in opposite directions, yet punishing anyone who comes between them.' (Sydney Smith)

Men are April when they woo, December when they wed: maids are May when they are maids, but the sky changes when they are wives. (William Shakespeare, *As You Like It*)

Let me not to the marriage of true minds
Admit impediments. (William Shakespeare, *Sonnet 116*)

It is a woman's business to get married as soon as possible, and a man's to keep unmarried as long as he can. (George Bernard Shaw)

Like fingerprints, all marriages are different. (George Bernard Shaw)

Marriage is popular because it combines the maximum of temptation with the maximum of opportunity. (George Bernard Shaw)

Marriage is like life in this – that it is a field of battle, and not a bed of roses. (Robert Louis Stevenson)

Marry on Monday for health.
Tuesday for wealth.
Wednesday for the best day of all.
Thursday for losses.
Friday for crosses.
Saturday no luck at all. (Traditional)

The best part of married life is the fights. The rest is merely so-so. (Thornton Wilder, *The Matchmaker*)

(See also Second marriage)

Medicine

The art of medicine consists of amusing the patient while nature cures the disease. (Voltaire)

Doctors bury their mistakes.

I am dying from the treatment of too many physicians. (Alexander the Great)

God heals and the doctor takes the fee. (Benjamin Franklin)

Doctors are lucky. The sun sees their successes – the earth covers their mistakes. (Greek saying)

Memory

Nothing is more responsible for the good old days than a bad memory. (Frank P. Adams)

Memory is the diary we all carry about with us. (Oscar Wilde)

Men and women

The women in this country are right good, pleasant, humble, discreet, sober, chaste, obedient to their husbands, true, secret, steadfast, ever busy, never idle, temperate in speaking and virtuous in all their works. Or at least they should be so. (William Caxton, *The Dictes and Sayings of the Philosophers*)

Once a woman has forgiven her man, she must not reheat his sins for breakfast. (Marlene Dietrich)

The great question which I have never been able to answer is, 'What does a woman want?' (Freud)

Men have sight, women insight. (Victor Hugo)

If men knew what women really think, they'd be ten times more daring. (Alphonse Karr)

The female of the species is more deadly than the male. (Rudyard Kipling, *The Female of the Species*)

Any man who says he can see through women is missing a lot. (Groucho Marx)

The test of a man or woman's breeding is how they behave in a quarrel. (George Bernard Shaw)

It is assumed that the woman must wait, motionless, until she is wooed. That is how the spider waits for the fly. (George Bernard Shaw)

First, then, a woman will, or won't, – depend on it;
If she will do it, she will; and there's the end of it. (Aaron Hill)

Mining

O the collier lad, he's a canny lad. (Johnny Handle, *The Coal-filler's Song*)

Misfortune

Misfortune arrives on horseback but departs on foot.

Monarchy

Monarchy is the oldest profession in the world. (Prince Charles)

Money

What is not needed is dear at a farthing. (Cato)

There is no fortress so strong that money cannot take it. (Cicero)

Money makes money and the money money makes makes money. (Benjamin Franklin)

Whatever you have, spend less. (Dr Samuel Johnson)

Get money; still get money, boy;
No matter by what means. (Ben Jonson)

Money is like a sixth sense with which you cannot make use of the other five. (W. Somerset Maugham)

Mothers

A mother is a mother still,
The holiest thing alive. (Samuel Taylor Coleridge)

For a wife take the daughter of a good mother. (Thomas Fuller)

Lincoln said, All that I am, or hope to be, I owe to my angel mother.

A mother's love endures through all; in good repute, in bad repute, in the face of the world's condemnation, a mother still loves on, and still hopes that her child may turn from his evil ways, and repent; she ... remembers the infant smiles ... the joyful shout of childhood, and the ... promise of his youth; and she can never be brought to think him all unworthy. (Washington Irving)

The hand that rocks the cradle ... rules the world. (William Ross Wallace)

Music

Where words fail, music speaks. (Hans Christian Andersen)

He who sings scares away his woes. (Miguel de Cervantes)

Music hath charms to soothe a savage breast. (William Congreve)

Music is the universal language of mankind. (Henry Wadsworth Longfellow, *Outre Mer*)

If music be the food of love, play on. (William Shakespeare, *Twelfth Night*)

Opinion

It is only about things that do not interest one that one can give a really unbiased opinion, which is no doubt the reason why an unbiased opinion is always valueless. (Oscar Wilde)

Parents

This would be a better world for children if parents had to eat the spinach. (Groucho Marx, *Animal Crackers*)

Patience

In any contest between power and patience, bet on patience. (W. B. Prescott)

Police

A policeman's lot is not a happy one. (W. S. Gilbert)

Praise

Let another man praise thee and not thine own mouth. (Old Testament)

Promises

Promises and pie crust are made to be broken. (Jonathan Swift)

Public speaking

Sometimes the difference between a good speaker and a poor speaker is a comfortable nap. (O. A. Battista)

It usually takes me more than three weeks to prepare a good impromptu speech. (Mark Twain)

You'd scarcely expect one of my age
To speak in public on the stage
And if I chance to fall below
Socrates or Cicero
Don't view me with a critic's eye
But pass my imperfections by.
Large streams from little fountains flow
Tall oaks from little acorns grow. (David Everett – adapted)

Quality

It's quality that counts, not quantity. A fly lays more eggs than a hen.

Rain

When the heavens weep, the earth shall live. (Hawaiian proverb)

Reading

To read without reflecting is like eating without digesting. (Edmund Burke)

Sailing and the Sea

I must go down to the seas again, to the lonely sea and the sky,
And all I as is a tall ship and a star to steer her by. (John Masefield)

they that go down to the sea in ships, that do business in great waters; these see the works of the Lord, and his wonder in the deep. For he commands, and raises the stormy wind, which lifts up the waves. Then they cry to the Lord in their trouble and he brings them out of their distress. He makes the storm calm, so that the waves are still. Then they are glad because they are quiet, and he brings them into their desired haven. (*Psalm 107*)

Second Marriage

To lose one husband is a misfortune. To lose two looks like carelessness. (Jane Austen)

We're number two. We try harder. (Avis car rental advertisement)

I'm not so old, and not so plain,
And I'm quite prepared to marry again. (W. S. Gilbert)

The triumph of hope over experience. (Dr Samuel Johnson)

When I lost my wife every family in town offered me another.

'Tis better to have loved and lost than never to have loved at all. (Alfred, Lord Tennyson)

And on her lover's arm she leant,
And round her waist she felt it fold,
And far across the hills they went
In that new world which is the old. (Alfred, Lord Tennyson)

Silence

Silence is the great art of conversation. (William Hazlitt)

Silence never makes mistakes. (Hindu proverb)

A closed mouth gathers no foot.

Silence is not always golden – sometimes it's guilt.

Success

Success is never final and failure never fatal. It's courage that counts.

On the day of victory no fatigue is felt. (Arabic proverb)

Man learns little from success, but much more from failure. (Arabic proverb)

The height of success in this world is having one's name written everywhere – except in the telephone directory. (Leo Chiosso)

Success is the child of audacity. (Benjamin Disraeli)

If at first you don't succeed, try, try, a couple of times more. Then quit: there's no sense in making a fool of yourself. (W. C. Fields)

There are two kinds of discontent in this world; the discontent that works and the discontent that wrings its hands. The first gets what it wants, and the second loses what it had. There is no cure for the first but success, and there is no cure at all for the second. (Elbert Hubbard)

Your own resolution to succeed is more important than any other one thing. (Abraham Lincoln)

There is no deodorant like success. (Elizabeth Taylor)

Television

Television is the third parent. (Buckminster Fuller)

Temptation

It's always hard to fight temptation. There is always the nagging thought that it might not happen again.

Time

Procrastination is the thief of time. (Edward Young, *Night Thoughts*)

Travel

I know where I'm going and I know who's going with me.

A man should know something of his own country, too, before he goes abroad. (Lawrence Stern)

In making up a party for a travelling excursion, always be sure to include one ignorant person who will ask all the questions you are ashamed to ask, and you will acquire a great deal of information you would otherwise lose. (Charles Dudley Warner)

Truth

Men occasionally stumble over the truth, but most of them pick themselves up and hurry off as if nothing had happened. (Winston Churchill)

Winter

Now is the winter of our discontent ... (William Shakespeare, *Richard III*)

Wisdom

Wisdom is knowledge tempered with judgement. (Lord Ritchie-Calder)

Work

Inspiration is to work every day. (Charles Baudelaire)

If you really want a job done, give it to a busy, important man. He'll have his secretary do it. (Calvin Coolidge)

One of the saddest things is that the only thing a man can do for eight hours a day, day after day, is work. You can't eat eight hours a day, nor drink for eight hours a day, nor make love for eight hours. (William Faulkner, *Writers at Work*)

To believe a business impossible is the way to make it so. (Fuller)

A verbal contract isn't worth the paper it's written on. (Sam Goldwyn)

The impossible is often untried. (Jim Goodwin)

When work is a pleasure, life is a joy! When work is a duty, life is slavery. (Maxim Gorky, *The Lower Depths*)

An invasion of ideas cannot be resisted. (Victor Hugo)

If you can keep your head when all about you are losing theirs, it is just possible that you haven't grasped the situation. (Jean Kerr, *Please Don't Eat the Daisies*)

If you have always done it that way, it is probably wrong. (Charles Kettering)

If hard work is the key to success, most people would rather pick the lock. (Claude McDonald)

Work expands to fill the time available for its completion. (C. Northcote Parkinson)

Worry

Blessed is the person who is too busy to worry in the daytime, and too sleepy to worry at night. (Leo Aikman)

Yesterday

Don't let yesterday take up too much of today. (Will Rogers)

9

DEFT DEFINITIONS

Definitions are very useful for inserting a little light relief into a speech. These are listed in subject order and are suitable for all types of speeches and presentations.

Abstinence

The thin edge of the pledge.

Absurdity

A statement of belief inconsistent with one's own opinion.

Acquaintance

Someone you know well enough to borrow from, but not well enough to lend to.

Adolescent

A teenager who acts like a baby when you don't treat him like an adult.

Advertising

The art of arresting human intelligence long enough to get money from it.

Anatomy

Something everybody has – but it looks better on a girl.

Appetizers

Little things you keep eating until you've lost your appetite.

Bachelor

A man with no ties – except those that need washing.

A man who has faults he doesn't know about yet.

Bank

A place that will lend you money if you can prove you don't need it.

Beach

A place where people slap you on the back and ask how you're peeling.

Blotting Paper

Something you search for while the ink dries.

Bore

Someone who talks when you want him to listen.

Someone who is here today, and here tomorrow.

Bottle

A container used for bringing up babies and bringing down adults.

Boxer

A man who hurts the one he gloves.

Bridge

A game of cards in which a good deal depends upon a good deal.

Bus

A vehicle that runs faster when you're after it than it does when you're in it.

Careful driver

One who has just spotted the police speed trap.

Coincide

What you do when it starts raining.

Collision

When two motorists go after the same pedestrian.

Congratulations

Sugar-coated envy.

Cough

Something which you yourself can't help but which everyone else does to annoy you.

Courage

The art of being the only one who knows you're scared to death.

Credit card

What you use to buy today what you can't afford tomorrow while you're still paying for it yesterday.

Critic

Someone who is quick on the flaw.

Someone who goes along for deride.

Criticism

Something you can avoid by saying nothing, doing nothing, and being nothing.

Culture

A thin veneer easily soluble in alcohol.

Cynic

A man who looks down on people above him.

A man who regards getting engaged as a first step towards a divorce.

Dancing

The art of pulling your feet away faster than your partner can step on them.

Desk

A waste-paper basket with drawers.

Diagnosis

Inside information.

Doctor

The only man who enjoys poor health.

Drip

Someone you can always hear, but never turn off.

Drunk

A person who drinks like a fish, but who would be better off if he drank only what a fish does.

Duty

Something one looks forward to without pleasure, does with reluctance, and boasts about afterwards.

Economist

One who knows how to throw money he/she hasn't got after the money he/she never had.

One who tells you what to do with your money after you've done something else with it.

Economy

Going without something you want in case you should sometime want something you probably don't want.

Efficiency expert

Someone who kills two birds with one stone – and gets the stone back.

One who waits to make up a foursome before going through a revolving door.

Egotist

One who is always me deep in conversation.

Escalator

Stairway to the stores.

Expert

One who takes a subject you already know and makes it sound confusing.

Fashion

Something which goes out of style as soon as everyone has one.

Something which goes in one year and out the other.

Free speech

Using someone else's telephone.

Fungi

The life and soul of the party.

Garden

Something most people prefer to turn over in their minds.

Genius

Someone who shoots at something that no-one else can see, and hits it.

Gentleman

A true gentleman is a man who knows how to play the bagpipes – but doesn't.

Girdle

The difference between fact and figure.

Golf

A long walk punctuated with disappointments.

Gossip

Something that runs down more people than cars.

Letting the chat out of the bag.

Harp

A naked piano

Hollywood

A place where a woman takes a man for better for worse but not for keeps.

Home

Place where a man can say what he likes – because no-one takes any notice of him anyway.

Horsepower

Something that was much safer when only horses had it.

Hypochondriac

Someone who enjoys pill health.

Impossible

Something that nobody can do – until somebody does it.

Inflation

A way of cutting a five pound note in half without damaging the paper.

Influence

Something you think you have until you try to use it.

Insurance

Something that keeps you poor all your life so that you can die rich.

Intermittent

A romantic proposal when camping.

Leadership

The art of getting someone else to do something you want done because he wants to do it.

Motorist

Someone who keeps pedestrians in good running order.

Necessity

A luxury that you bought on hire purchase.

Nudist

Someone who suffers from clothestrophobia.

Nudist camp

A place where men and women air their differences.

Pedestrian

Someone who was certain there was petrol in the tank even though the gauge registered empty.

Police helicopter

A whirlybird that catches the worm.

Prune

A plum that worried a lot.

Punctuality

The art of assessing how late the other person is going to be.

Race horse

The only creature that can take thousands of people for a ride at the same time.

Reality

A delusion created by an alcohol deficiency.

Recession

A period when we have to go without things our grandparents never heard of.

Riding

The art of keeping the horse between you and the ground.

Road map

Something that tells a motorist everything he wants to know – except how to fold it up again.

Scandal

Something that has to be bad to be good.

School

Place where kids catch colds from each other so they can stay at home.

Sneeze

Much achoo about nothing.

Solicitor

A man who makes sure that you get what's coming to him.

Sore throat

Hoarse and buggy.

Split second

The time between the lights changing and the driver behind you honking his horn.

Tact

The ability to describe others as they see themselves.

Taxpayer

The cross section of the public.

Television

An electric device which, when broken, stimulates conversation.

Towel

One of those little things sent to dry us.

Vegetarian

Someone who is nice to meat.

Vice versa

Poetry that is not suitable for children.

Will power

The ability to eat just one salted peanut.

GENERAL INDEX

SUBJECT INDEX

For Anecdotes, Definitions, Jokes, Proverbs and Quotations